Spectral Realms

No. 4 ‡ Winter 2016

Edited by S. T. Joshi

The spectral realms that thou canst see
With eyes veil'd from the world and me.

"To a Dreamer," *H. P. Lovecraft*

SPECTRAL REALMS is published twice a year by Hippocampus Press, P.O. Box 641, New York, NY 10156 (www.hippocampuspress.com). Copyright © 2016 by Hippocampus Press. All works are copyright © 2016 by their respective authors. The cover, "Prisoner (Head)" by Botond Reszegh is used by kind permission of the artist. Acrylic on canvas, 79 × 60 in., 2015. www.reszeghbotond.ro Cover design by Barbara Briggs Silbert. Hippocampus Press logo by Anastasia Damianakos.

ISBN 978-1-61498-161-9   ISSN 2333-4215

Contents

Poems 5
    The Phosphorescent Fungi / *D. L. Myers* 6
    Bone Fences / *Christina Sng* 7
    The Stain / *John Mundy* 8
    Relative Dark / *M. F. Webb* 10
    The Merlin of the Suns / *Liam Garriock* 12
    Who Knocks? / *Scott Thomas* 14
    The Flower Maidens / *David Barker* 15
    The Ghosts of Hyperborea / *Wade German* 16
    The Moon-Gate / *Ann K. Schwader* 17
    Machen Spoke the Hidden Thing / *John Shirley* 18
    Deeper Flowers Thrive / *Oliver Smith* 21
    With a Love So Vile / *Ashley Dioses* 24
    A Lone Figure / *Mary Krawczak Wilson* 25
    The Adverse Star / *Leigh Blackmore* 26
    The Vipers' Lament / *Jeff Burnett* 27
    Divine Marriage Comedy / *Alan Gullette* 28
    And Only Then I Saw / *Charles Lovecraft* 29
    Up the Stairs / *Alicia Cole* 30
    A Witch She Is / *William F. Nolan and Jason V Brock* 31
    The Stone of Sacrifice / *Kyla Lee Ward* 32
    Metamorphosis / *Christina Sng* 36
    Phantom / *Claire Smith* 37
    The Question / *Ian Futter* 38
    Someone Coming / *F. J. Bergmann* 40
    Absinthia / *K. A. Opperman* 41
    Lucinda the Killed / *Reiss McGuinness* 42
    The Yellow Jester / *John Thomas Allen* 44
    The Witch's Cat / *Pat Calhoun* 45
    Fiddler Jack / *Adam Bolivar* 46
    Caressa's Song / *David Barker* 56

The Procession / *M. F. Webb*	58
The Lovely Place / *John Mundy*	60
Gargoyles for the Cathedral / *Kendall Evans*	62
Flyover States / *Steven Withrow*	63
Bedtime Story / *Chad Hensley*	64
Zombification / *Alicia Cole*	65
Souls of Samhain / *Leigh Blackmore*	66
Ilvaa / *Ashley Dioses*	68
We Who Have Encountered Monsters / *Darrell Schweitzer*	70
Missed Horizons / *Ann K. Schwader*	71
The Ghost of Samhain Past / *Margaret Curtis*	72
The Poetry of Evil Must Never Be Shouted / *Darrell Schweitzer*	74
The Rise of Set / *Liam Garriock*	75
The Living Dead / *Ian Futter*	76
To My Goddess, Nicnevin / *Liam Garriock*	78
Deacon Mercer / *Jonathan Thomas*	80
Alastor / *Wade German*	84
Weird Tale / *Charles Lovecraft*	85
Among the Gargoyles / *K. A. Opperman*	86
The Girl with Pennies on Her Eyes / *Scott Thomas*	87
The Reunited / *Oliver Smith*	88
Graveyard Circumspect / *Alan Gullette*	91
Fog of War / *Christina Sng*	92
Two Fates / *John Mundy*	95
Alchemy / *Ian Futter*	96
Werewolf / *K. A. Opperman*	98
Panos / *Fred Phillips*	101
Water Tears / *Mary Krawczak Wilson*	102
The Summons / *David Barker*	103
The Witching Hour / *Alicia Cole*	104

Classic Reprints 105
   St. Irvyne's Tower / *Percy Bysshe Shelley* 107
   His Dream / *W. B. Yeats*.. 109
   Cthulhu / *David E. Schultz* 110
Articles.. 111
   The Poets of *Weird Tales*: Part 1/ *Frank Coffman* 113
Reviews 119
   In the Court of Hades / *Adam Bolivar* 121
   Enlightenment from the Outer Dark / *Donald Sidney-Fryer*............. 126
   Two Centuries of Pleasing Terrors / *Steven J. Mariconda*................. 134
Notes on Contributors 138

Poems

The Phosphorescent Fungi

D. L. Myers

A crawling darkness pressed upon my eyes
    In which a moiling sea of phantoms swam,
    And crazed, I hungered for a numbing dram
To send my mind to where all reason flies.
Until before me rose a fitful fire,
    A corpse-light foul and bruised that chilled my soul
    Yet drew me onward toward a ghastly goal—
A grotto burning like a purple pyre!

And then I saw the things that cast that glow,
    Pale fungi vile and stained with rank decay;
And bathed in icy sweat from head to toe,
    I stood and quaked before that dire display.
Then evil whispers hissed about my ears,
And I broke down in horror wracked with tears.

Bone Fences

Christina Sng

Six times stronger than steel
And easily obtainable anywhere,
She mastered carving on her own,
Her garage set up to debone carcasses.

After bleach and a bit of sun,
The bones were ready for use.
It was most popular for fences
With weatherproofing and

A thick coat of paint.
Passersby admired the unique
Shapes of the fences and
The strength of the thin material.

Her business boomed
Till the day someone ran a truck
Into a bone fence and screamed
When the panels split in two

And spilled their marrow.

The Stain

John Mundy

It was the merest blotch on my bedroom ceiling, a water stain from a treacherous roof. Surely nothing more. But it *grew* . . . and changed. And over many months it seemed to exert an unhealthy influence on my imagination. I had begun to perceive aspects, certain *troubling* aspects, in this accidental and freakish *Rorschach* that disturbed my peace of mind and soon tormented my dreams. Without conscious intent, night after night, as I lay sweating and turning in bed, my eyes were irresistibly drawn to it. It had begun to interfere with my solitary habits such as reading or merely indulging in harmless bits of fantasy before finally turning out the lights and embracing once-blessed sleep. Now, even sleep was poisoned by this Contagion and dreams had become terrible things. In my imagination, it had begun to resemble a face—not merely the ordinary distorted fancy of a face the mind inevitably reads into such accidental things, but a monstrous and distorted visage of inexpressible vileness, a mask of terrible and exquisite malignity. Night after night it leered down at me, until finally even sleep was but a fond memory. My imagination had *memorized* this taint in some terrible fashion, and now even in utter darkness it tortured me. The very awareness of its physical existence maddened me. Finally, I could endure no more and I rushed to my cellar, to return with the tools necessary to obliterate it forever. I succeeded; and the face, so horrible and unforgiving, was no more. Only fresh paint greeted my gaze.

But . . . *it troubles me still.* The paint *removed;* it did not *silence.* The mad laughter ceased after some weeks, but now—far worse!—the ghastly whispers, gentle but stern, alternating with the unyielding *croaking* admonishments, demanding *me* to justify my actions . . .

When will it be silent?

Relative Dark

M. F. Webb

It was many a generation ago,
    In a city not far from the sea,
That you drew forth from your own abyss
    Phantasms that deviously
Whisper e'en down to the present day
    A red brimming legacy.

Bells that chime in the maelstrom,
    The pendulum of the sea,
Dreams purloined from the ether,
    A cask and an addressee—
Ghosts and abominations
    That never my heart may flee.

Are you the reason I took up my pen
    In a desert century?
Where devils bred in the sandstorms
    And the winds took hold of me;
And though I fled from their madness
    They call incessantly,
Clamoring still from the pages
    In my home here by the sea.

You and I both with our papers,
    Our tortoise-shell cats and the sea,
And blood-deep demons to cruelly pursue,
    Pointing us perilously
To pen our abominations—
    A kinship that devils me,

For this blood it calls louder than mortal blood
    Through time and the dark, dark sea—
    Deeper by far than the sea—
And neither the angels nor imps can break
    Your ineffable legacy,
For you have reached through the ages
    And gripped my own century;

And never I sleep without feeling the seep
    Of a presence of chill degree,
Or I lie awake and I turn and shake,
    Unable to will myself free
From the demon who scolds as its fears enfold
    In a yearning threat of a night foretold—
What does it know of me, of me?
    Is it you that it seeks in me?

The Merlin of the Suns

Liam Garriock

For George Sterling

Haunted by the songs of the eternal stars
From boyhood, and the supernal beauty
Of the alien planets afloat in Infinity,
He sought the red desolation of Mars
And the Satanic seduction of Venus.
He, a cowled magician with magic glass,
Peered on visionary worlds diabolical and fabulous,
And recorded the suns and systems that pass
Into the black dread Vast, the ultimate Fear
That haunts every life-infested sphere
From red Arcturus to wise Aldebaran.
But in his odessey across space
He discovered the finite fate of Man,
The stark insignificance of the human race;
And so the hellish curse
Of the empty, cold universe
Descended upon him; but he was drawn
To other marvels, the inquisitive faun
That he was, and he unleashed his Fancy
To explore rich hothouses of evil flowers
And awaken stark, demoniac Powers
That answer to the crimson gods of sorcery.
Eventually after all the explorations

Across Imagination and the faery visions,
The Prophet of the Suns departed
To another existence altogether, to the uncharted
Realm beyond his beloved stars and suns
To escape the wraiths and legions of oblivions.
So let us salute the bold mage
Who showed us the heart of the cosmos,
Who travelled to where no man but poet ever goes.
Let us salute the immortal Merlin-sage.

Who Knocks?

Scott Thomas

Who knocks, I inquire
As I by the hearth retire.
Do branches and the wind conspire?
Does something rustle in the briar?
Do twigs snap in their pain of fire?

What hand knocks to chill inspire
And rakes the wood with nails of wire?
Whose voice that melancholy choir?
Who knocks at this ungodly hour?

The Flower Maidens

David Barker

Bee swarms effervesce,
in clouds coalesce,
in gardens of abandoned desire,
while pulpy blossoms conspire
gratification's delay
in a languid display
of burgeoning tumescent desire,
in their most damning floral attire.

Inquire of the flowers
their hypnotic powers,
when the moon is at its height
in the luminous pollen-rich night,
and they'll whisper a song
of the saffron-headed throng
rippling in the blazing star light,
waving in the numinous night.

The shapely flower lasses
who sprout from the grasses
while the hills are drenched in moon glow,
as the saps of the succulents flow,
exude fragrance alluring
to those not demurring,
enticing with narcotic delights
as verdant floral passion ignites.

The Ghosts of Hyperborea

Wade German

Beyond the polar region's death-white plain,
Black monoliths, like giant sentries, seem
To guard the limits of a lost domain
Amid eternal snows and glacial gleam—
Where ghosts, who took strange glory to their graves,
Now walk forever on the winds that rage,
And whisper of weirds from their forgotten age
Before Atlantis sank beneath the waves.

The spirits here were giants in their day—
Great conquerors, whose names were raised in chants
By evil slaves and holy hierophants . . .
But of their chronicles, now none can say.
The bitter, boreal winds that ever gust
Have long-since blown their epitaphs to dust.

The Moon-Gate

Ann K. Schwader

Set into some forgotten garden wall
between two desolations, it defies
the curious with cryptic glyphs that rise
& shimmer into twilight. Hardly tall
enough for use, its lunar curve betrays
no age or origin—the very stone
contributing a riddle of its own
in fossil traces faint as spectral haze.

Stout chains are strung at sunset to deny
all possibility of passage to
oblivion. On nights when only stars
illuminate our firmament, the sky
inside reveals a weirdly silvered view:
the moon this gate encloses is not ours.

Machen Spoke the Hidden Thing

John Shirley

His pale hands
divide
the lobes of my brain—
I paid a hundred
in gold
to be an hour insane;
and for pleasure like a red, red
symphony;
all the while it makes
a jest of me.
And the sage remembers
the hidden thing,
When Machen said:
(says though he's dead)—
"True evil is a rose that sings . . ."
"True evil is a rose that sings."

My flesh howls
with microscopic lips
My nerves vibrate
in cellular crypts;

Singing "Evil . . ."
". . . is a rose that sings . . ."
(True evil is a rose that sings . . .)

No matter how bright
falls the light
across icy stone walls;
no matter how warm
the fire burns—
still I feel it all:
I feel the uncast shadow fall;
feel the uncast shadow fall . . .

And all is seen through
a fog that rises
from invisible seas;
And the tempter comes
an hour past midnight;
Comes with hands
stretched out to me;
Singing True Evil is a Rose that sings;
True Evil is a Rose that sings . . .

   * * *

He's glib, he's charming—
like a travel agent
for Babylon.
His fingers are long
and cool, and white—
and very strong and very strong and very strong—
AND VERY STRONG.

For True evil . . .
is a rose that sings.
Machen spoke
of the hidden thing:
"True evil is a rose that sings . . ."
  True evil is a rose that sings.

Deeper Flowers Thrive

Oliver Smith

Once she dreamed among the deeper flowers:
The firstborn Eve. She slept in the shade
Of ancient vines and shadow-trees
Where sabled apple, dark lily, and hadean rose
Bowed heads, that dripped opiate-honey nectar
And thrived,
    In adoration of her hunger.

The jewel dusted skin of her unearthly face
Was suspended bright and still
Where other gods had cast her.
She lay a curse on the lip of all-hell's deep.
But with new aeons woke unbound,
Her face reflected
    In a world of darker waters.

Under the whirling dance of future stars,
Beneath the ships, moon, mackerel, and weed.
Among sailors who sank before Egypt rose
She is a pale figure swimming,
Unfurling eyes of blood, and fire,
Rising in forests,
    Where deeper flowers thrive.

Among the wrecks, sponges, and sulphur worms.
Abroad in the neon-glow of sea carved cloisters,
Bowers, basalt statues, and inflorescent life.
Nurtured in decay that falls as snow, as rain, as dust
From sunlight on green waves through blue to black.
Sediment accumulated,
    As league deep muck

Burying mysterious and half-ruined spires,
Magnificent in the ocean's gorgeous dream.
In gardens of gelatinous phantasmagoria
Some other lily, some other rose, some other vine
Some other bud that blooms to offer hungry lips
In abyssal groves,
    Where deeper flowers thrive.

The white-star eye among carven temple stone
Where whales drop like autumn fruits;
And serpent-spined fish writhe
Through rot, bone, blubber, and pale phosphorescence.
The dreamer slips silent through the darkness
To gather dehiscent flesh,
    Where deeper flowers thrive.

As tides wash down drowned lands, across dead planes
She swims in the wake of the all-consuming wave,
Gnawing on the bones of the conquered gods.
The first Eve rules as last Eve, over all who fall
Beneath the water, willing and supine; who desire
Lips that whisper,
    How deeper flowers thrive.

With a Love So Vile

Ashley Dioses

For D. L. Myers

The Oracle treads the land with grace and stealth.
Remnants of mist trail fleetingly away
As, nourishing the nightshade blooms in wealth,
At night he waits for a life to decay.
Few silver strands of wisdom touch his face
As claws of wind wisp by that dare to play.
He is a man above the human race,
Yet his cold heart has found one like the fae.
And with a love so vile, so soon, he savors
Her sweetened torment and her screams like songs.
With matchless beauty, the great Oracle favors
Her pain to joy, until for death she longs.

A Lone Figure

Mary Krawczak Wilson

In Antarctica, I saw a lone figure—like a filament
Estranged from a barely blooming flower.
It beckoned me and then the skies erupted in a shower;
Words were whispered in the wind, but I knew not what they meant.

Soon the snows flattened the grim horizon
And only a black dot appeared on a blank white page,
Uttering and echoing its pain and rage
Of its impotence and terror after losing the warmth from the sun.

Then the snow subsided and left in its wake an inkblot
Erasing even the infinitesimally solitary figure
Who now blended into the icy whitening blur,
Deadened from a fight that was never fought.

For this unearthly place, as seen from afar,
Sheds its flickering light
Only on moonless nights
When lone figures roam from the abattoir.

The Adverse Star

Leigh Blackmore

Unclouded moon lofts high above the bar
And seems to sigh and signal where you are;
It is a thing unseemly and bizarre,
The rulership of this most Adverse Star

That blinks beside the moon and casts wan light
From gulphs uncrossed, and makes your skin glow white.
The Adverse Star is glinting there this night;
I wish it were not half so deathly bright!

The fateful course that set us on our way
Has taken us from hearth and home; dismay
And lost desire; storm-wrack blots the day
In motionless embrace; all seems passé.

The cracks of time now in our voices are
As we lament the heavenly vision far
And strum our sad and lonely old guitar
Beneath the baleful light—that Adverse Star!

The Vipers' Lament

Jeff Burnett

". . . on sounding wings hovered a conqueror in the fluent air, over sands, Libyan, where the Gorgon-head dropped clots of gore, that, quickening on the ground, became unnumbered serpents; fitting cause to curse with vipers that infested land."

—Ovid, *Metamorphoses*

A crimson shower slakes the burning sands;
The conqueror fiend incarnadines the dunes
With the fruitful blood of the pallid, snake-locked moon:
Future venoms sired by his hand.
Congealing on the paths of caravans
A morphing brood of deadly vipers horned,
Sprung from the clotted drops of Gorgon gore:
Miracles no Olympian can remand.

The orphans coil beneath the burnt-orange sea,
Impervious to the red siroccos driven
By ancient Typhon's sere and cindery breath;
Cyclones churn with the dolor of the riven
Tongues that hiss sonorous threnodies
For the Serpent Queen, the Mother fecund in Death.

Divine Marriage Comedy

Alan Gullette

Like Beatrice I shape her
From frozen mood rings and sundae supplements,
Rouge of sugarplum, lipstick of sentiment,
    orphan eyes.

Like Daphne I drape her
In cellophane, then bind her in cerements
Of gazeux-soaked gauze and the drippings of
    ceremonial candles.

Like Gwendolyn I take her:
Standing together between the square teeth of the battlement,
I take her as we fall, entwined in a slow,
    spiraling descent . . .

And like Echidna at last I stake her,
Watching with Typhon as she labors on rocks awash with afterbirth . . .
In a swirling cloud, the Firebirds rise to fulfill
    our destiny.

And Only Then I Saw

Charles Lovecraft

I walked the moon tall sky with lower cloud
Like fairy hills in glens of bearing gold.
I watched as the ancestor stars took hold
Of my imaginings in roarings loud.
Throughout my mind lone pockets of the dark
Now blended in the voids' apocalypse,
And rose then high in fevers of strange trips
To dance where alien thresholds made their mark.

All these wild things I saw and felt, the frieze
Of distances beyond control, and knelt
Where blossoms of vast spirals peep in svelte
And from the peace of night weave symphonies
Fit for star folk to amble in, to their
Appointed realms . . . on which we can but stare.

Up the Stairs

Alicia Cole

Old and cantankerous: a
snarling mass of teeth.
Her chattering bones like
the knotty rasping
of tree limbs.

And then, the Gremlin.
The death waiting inside—
her, the casing; her, the
flesh tightening around
her last flight.

Up the stairs. The
Gremlin's teeth bright
like the moon scudding
hard against the horizon.
Then, going out.

A Witch She Is

William F. Nolan and Jason V Brock

She lives alone,
This gloomy creature—
Alone in the woods.

Spiders avoid her,
Needle-tailed scorpions
Turn away;
She dwells in shadow—
Without light, lamp, or candleshine—
Inside her abode austere,
Accompanied only by familiars
Creeping strange,
At home in the woods.

A witch she is,
Casting eldritch spells
Upon those who dare to venture near;
Haunting the gallows,
Compiling her grimoire, biding time
Within her hovel severe—
Serenaded by toads, she is comforted by fear
and does not change,
Alone in the woods.

At home in the woods,
This gloomy creature—
She lives alone.

The Stone of Sacrifice

Kyla Lee Ward

You may well wonder how the stone survived.
Wasn't it destroyed? Wasn't it cast down
when soldiers sanctified by shot and steel
arrived to slaughter its red-handed priests
and sacked their city, melted down their gold?
And how could it endure the missionaries
that raised their cross upon the temple steps?
Then followed the accretion of clay brick,
of roads and rails, and concrete at the last.

But you can tell it's real, even through glass.
This complex of conditioned air and light
is fashioned to preserve and yet display.
Secure, it glows like embers, like a jewel.
Yet to the first who dared the scoriac peaks,
it was much more. To come upon a plug
of crimson midst the black obsidian!
The Gods had made the world from their own blood
and these men had the wit to know a scab.

They gave their blood to carve it. Water, sand,
and wooden drills propelled by human hand
created faces: yes, those things are faces.
The numinous equipped with teeth and tongue.
And yet, it was the natural shape of stone
that gave the rite. And now you feel surprise
that it should be so small. The surgeon's slide
and mortuary slab inform your thoughts:

this is no bed. A prop beneath the back.
To kneel and lean, and show, is no despite:
it is a gift. Surrendering this way
the warrior returns to infancy.
Priests held them down, but did you know they spoke?
For priest and victim shared the potent draught,
receiving visions of the world to come.
The victim's words were hearkened over all,
for he gazed upwards to the sovereign sun.
The priest gazed down. Through skin and ribs, into
the ever-beating heart within all things.

How many died upon this whorl of rock?
The legends say that twenty thousand men
gave up their lives when first the stone was set.
And thence the sacred year progressed serene
a hundred times, from planting to the pick.
Each season duly paid in mortal blood
to granting sky and all-succouring earth.
And this was known: the missionaries took
confession of their captives, heard their songs
and saw the figures carved upon the walls;
recorded all, so their achievement might
be measured by the horror overcome
so deftly. How then did the stone survive?
An adept would already know the truth.

* * *

They must have laughed, the faithful that remained,
to hear the new God asked no sacrifice:
that blood was not the germ of this new world.
Twelve times the dedication was surpassed
as soldiers slew and plague raged through the streets—
a sacrifice of unimagined zeal!
The stone, not broke but buried by the new,
by duelling ground, the gallows tree and gaol;
the stone, rejoined to earth, accepted these
new rites, and over time the Gods drank deep.
Adjusted to a hectic calendar
where sacrifice could come at any time.
Came to accept exchange of weak for strong,
impure for perfect. So the stone endured;
became, unseen, foundation of a state.
Until the day it saw the light once more.
An accident, they say, while laying wire.

And do you think they stripped the stains away,
when first they placed it on its rubber bed?
And now they ship it off to foreign shores:
they say this tour encompasses the world.
A gesture of goodwill, of cultural pride,
a nation claiming space upon that stage
where each competes in curiosities.

A round stone, carved with angular grotesques
and glyphs no one can read. That draws your eye,
your steps across the floor. You know it's real
and whether you believe my tale, or no,
you can't deny that there is power here.
Perhaps there is, you say. But no one now
shall feed the Gods. There's nowhere left today
where people make a rite of murdering,
inventing crimes to so condemn their own,
permit hot blood to saturate the ground,
send smoke into the sky and claim it good.
So you may say; I shake my head and smile,
and ask how you can possibly think that.

Metamorphosis

Christina Sng

My skin was burning.
It was time for the shedding.
For new skin to grow from the old.

Ten days and nights, I suffered
The great purge, violent itching
Both day and night.

Finally the skin peeled and fell
Into a pile of leathery dust.
From within, a new skin emerged

With fine fur and a series of spikes.
It's time, it's time, my mother cried,
And we all lined up in a row outside.

Our leader nodded when he saw
All of us and chirped once
As we took to the sky.

Phantom

Claire Smith

A stranger on the back stairs
Disappears into the wall with its flock
Flower pattern. She closes herself up, up tight,
Lost in the velvet; leaves hints of gold dust.

It's the start of a holiday game of hide and seek.
The girl scribbles pictures, writes stories,
Prints butterfly wings. Builds a pile
Of coloured lining-paper creations

All hidden in the old maids' quarters
Among dust, clutter, and cobwebs—
The leftovers from times lost.
Her friend flies away from the house for good

When autumn returns, at summer's end.
She escapes forever from its darker corners
Beyond the wall at the end of the garden
Clothed in brambles, buddleia, and bindweed,

To a chipped, flaked, and cracked shell.
A summer house—suitable coffin—
Place to disappear to. Place of peace.
A place to finally rest withered wings.

The Question

Ian Futter

If before my bawling birth,
when unbound spirits
bind to earth,
I'd been given the right to choose,

The right to choose
some seventy years of life,
then lose that life—
what would I choose?

To know the things
which I'd hold fast,
were never mine and wouldn't last.
What would I choose?

To know the stuff
for which I strive
could not this body keep alive.
What should I choose?

To feel with every fluttering breath
a mayfly's life and fossil death.
Why would I choose?

Why would I choose
to briefly spark
against cold ether's ceaseless dark?
Why would I choose?

And yet my momentary light,
like stars long dead,
may still glow bright.
So must I choose.

Someone Coming

F. J. Bergmann

There's always someone coming.
—First line from "Erik Satie Watusies His Way into Sound"
by Jeff Allessandrelli

He sits at his laptop, near a bright window,
steaming cup of coffee close by at a safe
distance from his keyboard. He enters bursts
of typing, his fingers cantering over the keys.
In between, he stares at what he's written,
on the screen. Outside, the winter light dims
to mauve, then violet, indigo, deeper, darker,
as his reflection in the window glass slowly
appears and sharpens. At full dark, his double
turns away from its own monitor, gazes at him
a while, and begins to speak. From the corner
of his eye he watches it smile, leaning in.

Absinthia

K. A. Opperman

She comes to me from out the emerald gloom
That gathers in the shadows of my room,
When I am nodding, drunk with sharp perfume—
The breath of absinthe from my crystal glass.

She is a languid, strange, smaragdine girl,
Whose verdant tresses flowingly unfurl.
Pale sprigs of mugwort weave her crown, and curl
Around bare arms that beck from dream's morass.

Her mouth of wormwood—ah, her bitter kiss!—
Delivers me into the green abyss.
Upon her bosom's herby couch, the bliss
Of poisonous nepenthe fills my soul.

Yet sweet Absinthia so soon is gone,
And in the liquor's cloudy celadon
I see a sad reflection, worn and wan—
A ghoulish thing deformed by time's grim toll.

Lucinda the Killed

Reiss McGuinness

I had not heard from her in weeks.
Neither her friends nor family knew where she was.
I was lingering like a ghost outside her house,
for the third night I knocked the front door, the back.
Suppose the lights came on,
suppose she answered, would she forgive a trick like this,
a sinner like me?
There are no bouquets of flowers,
no lines of Eliot that can apologise for this.

Through the back door I broke in.
Everything was left neat and tidy, unlived in,
but that is how she lived.
I called her name, turned the lights on,
the bleak rooms turning on one by one.
Up the stairs I crept, calling her name, listening for something,
knocked the doors of each bedroom;
each bed was still made.
I came out into the hallway and saw the door in the ceiling,
the attic, and considered the dark, unlit fibre glass floor.
Surely she could not be there . . .
I pulled the ball ended string handle,
pulled down the ladders, looked up to a naked light bulb
left on. I shouted her name as I climbed into the light,
at first, there was nothing, but then, a shadow

cutting the room in two caught me,
there; a stick-man tree branch with hair for leaves.

What else, but my now ex-girlfriend,
hanged in the attack, dead,
how the light caused your shadows to dance
as if you were being lit up from everywhere.

I recall you swinging there when I am freezing in the snow,
lying on your burial mound, ear to the ground,
listening for a message,
asking who they were, who it was,
"One with a blood-red pupil,
one with only one eye,
one with a fringe as black as tar,
ancient, starving, just took advantage
of the fact I wanted to die."

The Yellow Jester

John Thomas Allen

His face expands in oblong midnight,
the base of each point dissolving
in black mother-of-pearl pools.

His fingernails wind round synaptic
pipe cleaners in the brain's contorting
base, and in nightmares his pillars stand

rude with moonlight. Angels with narcotic
eyes roll in stone orbs of ether, and tiles
of trick satin rife with purple fuzz

gangrenous as his rumor pull back
in your drowning to reveal him,
leering, jaundiced, teeth numbered

in hexes of ashen cuneiform spinning
as your breast heaves once more,
and a sign forms in Yellow.

The Witch's Cat

Pat Calhoun

For Tiger

High above the village,
Streaking through the sky,
On her broom the witch rides,
And on her back ride I.

We split the night like lightning;
Our laugh fills folks with fear.
Deliriously happy
Together in the air,

We're as close as two can be.
I am her, and she is me.
I've watched her eat the mice she kills:
She has seen me casting spells.

They say that we are evil;
I know our hearts are dark.
But the black fire kept burning,
Once love gave it a spark.

And so we go a-riding.
But there's one thing I know:
If my beloved witch should die,
I'd be struck a mortal blow.

Fiddler Jack

Adam Bolivar

Jack Drake, the son of Hunter John,
Was not a hunter's son;
To something else was his heart drawn,
And all else did he shun.

Jack found a fiddle in the walls—
A vile rat showed him where—
With catgut for its purring strings,
A bow of horse's hair.

There was a daisy-dotted place
Where Jack would play unseen,
And to his father's great disgrace
They called it Fidder's Green.

So gently would Jack coax his strings
That even birds would hark,
And pixies streamed from underground
When daylight ebbed to dark.

The pixies danced beneath the trees;
They danced in twos and threes;
They spunanspunanspunan—whee!—
Like petals in the breeze.

A pixie-maid caught Jack's shy gaze,
And Myrrha she was called;
With cowslips in her golden hair,
The fiddler was enthralled.

'O golden hair, in verdant gown,
So beauteous to see,
O golden hair will you let down
Your golden hair for me?'

The fiddler's father feared for Jack,
That he should have a trade;
And many times he called his son,
And many times he say'd:

'My boy, come give me thy fiddle,
If e'er you mean to thrive.'
But Jack tossed back his tangled hair:
'Not to any man alive!

'If I my bow should cease to raise,
They'd think that I've gone mad!
For many are the joyous days
With music I have had.'

And Jack returned to Fiddler's Green
To play his witchy tune,
And pixies danced for him unseen
Beneath the milk-white moon.

'O I won't be my father's Jack,
And Myrrha is my Jill,
For she will be the fiddler's wife,
With music when she will.'

The slithy snake was jealous of
Fair Myrrha's love for Jack;
He bit her on her iv'ry heel—
I rue the day, alack!

Salt sorrow flow'd from Jack's blue eyes;
He cradled Myrrha's husk.
The mourning dove soft cooed a dirge
As night replaced the dusk.

'O woe, O woe,' wailed Fiddler Jack.
'My truelove now is gone.
My truelove now is far below,
But ashes now, and bone.'

A cat stepped out from someplace dark,
  Her fur was sleek and grey.
'I'll take you to the Land of Nod
  To try the King to sway.

'If you can lull him with your song,
  Your love he may return.
To you her soul does most belong;
  For you her heart does yearn.'

Rejoicing at the grey cat's news,
  Jack followed her in haste;
He journeyed to the Land of Nod,
  A gloomy rainy waste.

There only thorn and thistle grew,
  And mournful winds did moan.
Jack trod upon a tricksome path,
  A catwalk of wet stone.

A slack-jawed dog crouched at the gate,
  A snarling hungry ward.
The grey cat's fur stood on its end;
  Jack struck a soothing chord.

The dog left off its ugly growl
And yipped his love for Jack.
Jack tickled him beneath the chin
And didn't once look back.

The castle of the King was stark,
And open was the door;
No tapestries upon the walls,
No carpets on the floor.

The King sat on an onyx throne,
His Queen enthroned beside;
He had not slept for countless years—
To lull him scores had tried.

Jack doffed his goose a-feather'd hat,
A courtesy most clear;
And with a flourish poised his bow,
But played with little cheer.

The King's eyes glazed like window panes,
Whose drapes began to fall;
And over all the shadowed court
A lethargy did pall.

The pale Queen from her throne arose
And offered Jack a comb.
'Now tie your truelove's locks with this
And lead her to your home.

'But one thing must I warn you, Jack:
Until you see the day,
Don't look behind to see her face,
Or she will drift away.'

Behind the throne an aperture,
And through it Jack did slip;
A hermit met him in the dark,
And to Jack did he quip:

'My riddle hear, O Fiddler Jack:
My house without a door,
Its brittle walls would surely crack
If it should hit the floor.'

And to this test did Jack reply,
'The answer is quite plain;
I would be telling you a lie
To say it taxed my brain.'

The hermit lent sly Jack his lamp,
And Jack crept down the stair;
His blood was sluggish from the cold,
While fear pricked up his hair.

He passed then to a darkened wood
And followed glowing stones;
The lanthorn lit a ghastly pile
Of ghoulish well-gnawed bones.

A garden lay in front of Jack,
An iron fence around;
A garden where no roses grew,
But bramble did abound.

Beneath an elm a woman sat,
Her face hid by a veil;
She beckoned Jack to sit with her;
Before him was a grail.

She poured her tea into Jack's cup,
And then some for her own;
Jack took a sip and tasted blood,
And heard from far a moan.

Jack staggered from the garden gate
And wandered up a trail.
A woman wept at river's edge;
He heard her keening wail.

Cleft in the roof of stone a crack,
And through it there did shine
A single star upon the one
For whom poor Jack did pine.

'O Myrrha, dear, my only one,
I've come so far for you;
O Myrrha, bright, my only sun,
I've won such games for you;

'O Myrrha, pale, my only moon,
I'll only play for you;
I'll play this song, through nights so long,
For Myrrha, only you . . .'

Jack braided tight her golden locks
And fixed them fast to stay;
He pinned the knot with witch's comb,
And then he turned away.

He hurried up the glowing path
And shunned the sounds behind;
The darkness was so inky black
He felt that he was blind.

Jack clambered up the many steps
And paid the hermit's due;
He dared not glance behind his back,
Although he could construe.

The King and Queen were fast asleep;
The gate yawned open wide;
The sky was pink and forebode dawn,
But still did Jack abide.

From far away a cockcrow came;
Jack wheeled around in joy;
A single tear in Myrrha's eye
Did all his hopes destroy.

The mountain cock crowed mountain dawn,
And Myrrha turned to mist;
An Angell reckoned in his book
His Sisters' cruelest twist.

Bereft of rhyme and reason's gifts,
Jack turned back to his green,
Where pixies streamed from out of rifts
To dance for him unseen.

But Jack just sat upon his rock
And let his fiddle lay;
The pixies begged him for a tune,
But no more would he play.

They cracked the fiddle like an egg
Upon a cold hard stone;
And then they took the fiddler's arms
And rent them bone from bone.

They feasted on his liver's meat
And plucked out both his eyes;
They drank his blood like wine so sweet
And relished long his cries.

The pixies took the fiddler's head
And threw it in the Tay;
And down it drifted very far,
Still singing all the way:

'O golden hair, O golden hair,
I sung for thee, O golden hair.'

Caressa's Song

David Barker

"Betimes he doth consume these flowers,
knowing they shall bloom another day."
—*The Tablets of Nhing*

1.

One cold and foggy morning
the King beside the lake
met the fair Caressa,
her chastity to take.

He bid her to escort him,
concealing what he planned.
"Carcosa now awaits us."
He offered her his hand.

Demure, the maiden followed,
submitting to his lust.
She gave her virtue hallowed—
her heart knew only trust.

"Forever thee, I'll love," she sighed,
He called his guards; anon she died.

2.

Next spring the lake was thawed,
surrendering its dead,
and left upon the shore—
a corpse with yellow head.

The necrosed lass arose:
on withered limbs she strode
straight through a haunted wood
toward the King's abode.

By stealth of dark she gained
the Monarch's feathered bed;
and she lay down, a ghoulish bride,
as if they had been wed.

"Forever me you'll love," she sighed,
and terror-struck, he swiftly died.

The Procession

M. F. Webb

She thought them commonplace when she was small:
Harmonies that through the garden rang,
A flash of wing atop the farthest wall,
The day, perhaps, after a winter ball,
A lace of footprints where the fountain sprang.

She did not know that childhood had lent
A gift of understanding to her ears,
That life both troubled and magnificent
Would leave her for the greater part content,
But lose that scattered brilliance to the years

Till even memories were hard to find—
Although it seemed that something she had lost
Would try to scrawl itself across the rind
Of frost on windows bleak and winter-lined.
By waking light she might remark the cost,

But life itself is boon and sacrifice.
And rather than consort with such regret,
She told herself life's comforts would suffice
To compensate for any loss or price,
And she was glad of childhood's end. And yet—

(The ballroom dance upon a floor of ferns
A drift of music teasing at the ear)
She seems to catch a flicker as she turns.
And dares to wonder, even as she yearns—
If 'tis to only children they appear;

For on this morning cold and iron gray
She gathers up her bones to cross the floor,
Drawn by voices of a distant day—
A melody as if the Folk array
To sing her welcome just beyond the door.

The Lovely Place

John Mundy

The Garden was lovely—
Rare and forbidden.
A Place of fragrances,
of perfumes exquisite.
And oh, of such colors! Nuances
To shame the greatest of artists.
And the Flowers, the *Flowers*,
Their shapes the crowning glory!
Fantastic and outré
Like delicate internal organs
of small animals or children;
Like ropes of flesh they coiled
And uncoiled, looping endlessly
Over the stark white
Of bones, strange and ancient.
I visited it once
In the cold fall
Alone but not alone,
Feeling the stare of the very old folk
From their quaint weathered
Cottage, peering, peering
Through windows the vines
Had not yet swallowed.
I thought it then a peaceful place
To seek green rest and

Dream beautiful dreams.
So I rested and slept
And I dreamed
And only my bones screamed.

    –Inspired by Thomas Ligotti's "Flowers of the Abyss"

Gargoyles for the Cathedral

Kendall Evans

Captured from a realm
    of prowling grotesques
Brought down by a wizard's
    verbal arabesques

Monster-hunting mage
Wild, spell-statued gargoyles
Frozen in stone
Transported to the cathedral

Flyover States

Steven Withrow

Up in the contrails over South Dakota
I study blank irrigated rhombuses
and think of a revision Richard Feynman
shared with Lovecraft after two cancers killed him.
The physicist and writer spoke often now,
and they were walking the Providence streets,
moving downhill from Swan Point Cemetery
near the psychiatric hospital. "Howard,"
Feynman said, "my last words were not, as noted,
'I'd hate to die twice. It's so boring.' That's wrong.
Mine: 'Can't git away—draws ye—ye know summ'at's
comin' but tain't no use—'"
    "You flatter me, sir."
Lovecraft had not known his companion had read
"The Colour out of Space." He was gratified.
Below me, etchings in the Great Plains suggest
twin eye teeth pulled from the Cheyenne River's mouth.

Bedtime Story

Chad Hensley

Down a cold, shadowed street a dark house stands.
Under its creaking roof a mother sits
Reading to children who whisper demands,
Wishing to be scared out of their frail wits.
When she is through reading the children's tale
And several hours ago turned out the light,
The sleeping children awake, frightened pale
From dreams at the exact stroke of midnight.

They clutch their sheets, staring at a shadow
Moving behind their heads on the far wall,
Afraid to look across at the window,
Knowing they had better not scream at all.
Soon they shall whimper themselves back to sleep
While in their room the shadow continues to creep.

Zombification

Alicia Cole

There is a moment when the iron
jaws of irreversible change clang
shut, when horror takes hold.
A faint scraping in the brain.
The change becomes the blood's
rushing, and then the blood's
silence; then, a moment. The brain
not quite dead. But it is only
a moment, like the moon breaking
through thick clouds, then ceasing
to exist, engulfed. Only a moment,
then eternal roaring blankness.
Behind veils we walk, shuffling,
trying to taste life. Behind veils
we wake. Never tasting life again.

Souls of Samhain

Leigh Blackmore

When harvest ends and first frost's on the land
The Souls of Samhain show their spirit hand.
From summer pastures cattle are brought in,
Livestock are slaughtered; let winter begin!

Light up the hilltop bonfires! Feasts commence!
On All Souls' Night, the goblins hasten hence,
Revisiting their homes and living kin;
Dead otherworldly souls scream wail and din.

Since Tigernmas, the King to Crom Cruach,
Did sacrifice a child in horror stark,
Did smash its newborn head 'gainst idol-stone
To safeguard people, wintry land and throne,

The Souls of Samhain still we must appease—
Scatter the blackened ashes, if you please!
From winter's darkness and its dread decay
Bright bonfires, like the sun, protect the day.

Some welcome dining places don't forget,
And candles in your westward windows set
For Souls of Samhain who appear this night;
Use salt and iron should they give you fright.

This *danse macabre* will hear the churchbells ring.
Let's feast with apples, nuts, and everything!
Let's go in guise unto our neighbours' doors
With painted, veiled faces—Samhain's laws!

With decorated horse-skulls let us mum
Now that the year's dark half has swiftly come!
Let's take our cattle killed and freeze our meat
So through grim winter's length we still can eat!

The Souls of Samhain—do they mean us harm?
Appease them and the restless spirits calm.
The *Aos Si* will soon depart this earth;
Let's cheer them on their way with festive mirth!

Ilvaa

Ashley Dioses

The Silver Death, for now, has fled before this ring
Of strange red metal and black gems to suit a king.
The plague came down from Achernar, that brilliant star
That glares upon me without ceasing, from afar.
I am a realmless king with three surviving slaves,
And must in Cyntrom find my shelter, past the waves.
We crashed and then were captured by the island men.
That's when she came; and to their king they brought me then.

Her name was Ilvaa, and she wore vermillion skirts
And breast-cups of bright lazuli, fairest of flirts.
The girl upon me kindly smiled, yet led me to
The king of the dread Isle of Torturers and knew
That here I'd face my death instead of in my home.
The king sent me to rooms with views of ocean foam,
And devil-fish whose tentacles writhed on the walls,
And floating corpses, staring with their eyes' white balls.
With a soft haunting sorcery, her face returned.
For the first time in many suns, how my heart burned.

Aloft on his high brazen chair, the king sent me
To stand against cruel torture with scarce a plea!
The fumes of dragon gall and the adipocere
Of long-dead cannibals were burned together here,
Intoxicating both my lungs and breathing-way.
Yet Ilvaa tenderly regarded me today;
And when the torture ceased, she sneaked into my room,
And twin desires of love and life began to bloom.

She silkily caressed my wet, enfevered brow,
And rubbed oils on my burning limbs with a stern vow
To set me free; and I believed her whispered word.
Yet dawn approached and she awaited with the herd,
And snickered without any shame as I was bound
Upon the wheel of adamant; her wine was browned
With poisons, yet her blackened lie was my true pain.
I begged to keep my ring—my trick was not in vain!
The king was quick to seize it and the Silver Death
Then came for me and them and it stilled every breath.

   –After Clark Ashton Smith's "The Isle of the Torturers"

We Who Have Encountered Monsters

Darrell Schweitzer

What kind of survivors shall we become,
we who have encountered monsters,
escaped them, slain them, or come away
bearing monsters within us?
We know where the dark doors are.
We speak fluently the language of death.
We are past shame or hoping for pity.
The most picturesquely mutilated among us
have done their time as sideshow freaks.
We flaunt our scars proudly, ready to offend
because we know how very special we are.
We have, caged within our hearts,
that which yearns for havoc
and waits patiently for inevitable release.
Is this how it ends, then?
Do we become the monsters ourselves
and exist to terrify some new generation of victims?

Missed Horizons

Ann K. Schwader

Scant hours after nine-plus years. That's all
the time & treasure humankind could spare
to catch a glimpse of secrets seething there
at our creation's rim. If fungi crawl
across that pallid heart—unfurl their wings
in hydrocarbon haze—we may not know
for months. The data's streaming far too slow,
in packets yet to be unpacked. Dark things
deny themselves to science: no device
unaided by imagination knows
enough of Outside perils to expose
inhabitants beneath exotic ice.

Our calculations left too little space
for speculation past the most mundane
details of speed & fuel. With our brains
bewitched at this exhilarating pace,
distracted by fresh baubles in the black,
we glanced & hurried on. But what glanced back?

The Ghost of Samhain Past

Margaret Curtis

I dwell in darkness through the rolling year,
Except when stars come right, bright cracks appear.
My old eyes then I shield, and wend my way
Toward that flickering light 'twixt night and day.

I leap through time and space to land on earth,
Surrounded suddenly by howls of mirth
And shrieks of fear. Alas, 'tis ever thus
For modern humans seldom welcome us.

It was not always so. Once when I came
They stood prepared and called my sacred name.
They left me food and drink and danced for me.
But these days all is foolish fakery.

Except sometimes at Samhain, when I might
A circle find, of folk who still delight
In offering respect, and then I dance,
To celebrate this wondrous circumstance.

You in the World would do well to take heed:
We all have ancestors, beloved dead
Between the Worlds, your dear lost kith and kin,
To call upon when next the veil is thin.

And don't forget to leave an offering
Of food, or flowers fresh, recalling spring.
We shall commend your gifts to Samhain's ghost
When at life's end you pass and join our host.

The Poetry of Evil Must Never Be Shouted

Darrell Schweitzer

Keep in mind that all the fun stuff,
the screaming virgin on the altar at midnight,
the swirling demons conjured out of the air,
and, most especially, the endless orgies amid standing stones,
are mere show-biz for the weak-minded,
not much different from the incense and mummeries
used to fill a collection plate.
Real evil is much more subtle,
its poetry never to be shouted,
its negation like a stain
left behind by oily smoke.
It has to get behind the eyes,
penetrate the brain slowly until
you face the abyss absolutely, and feel nothing.
Only then are you ready to reach for the knife.

The Rise of Set

Liam Garriock

The nightmare: in a pyramid of night
    I saw stars twinkling in the desert skies
    Where Silence was broken by passing flies.
Then ancient guardians, stone failures, took flight
To warn the people of a divine light
    Of a vast Force that shall silence all cries
    And freeze the billion stars as all life dies
'Neath its inscrutable and searing might.

Fire burned the cities—humankind was gone;
    The waters dried up and the oceans froze,
        And the stars withered in the universe.
Our cindered Earth became its ashen throne;
    From perished systems a mournful wind blows
        To hail the Chaos' dire, eternal curse.

The Living Dead

Ian Futter

It took my life,
this thing.
It hauled me down.
It gouged my frown.
It chafed me.

It took my life,
this thing,
some thirteen years
and tranced my nowhere-wife
and tears
into a cipher.

This thing, with cold cathedral lies.
Chipped marbles; coloured glass
for eyes.
It ate me.

It fried the friends,
who I held dear.
Its blazing breath
burnt all things clear.
It made me.

And all my kids,
who might have been,
are empty bedrooms,
vacant, clean.

It took my life,
this thing.

To My Goddess, Nicnevin

Liam Garriock

With witches' jasper cup and rite
    I recite thy hag-worshipped name.
    Come, O come, Mistress of Elphame,
Come into the dark, haunted night!

Queen! deathly beauty incarnate:
    Hosts of ghosts accompany thee
    As thou, brooding, approachest me,
Who opened Hell's warlock-sealed Gate.

In thy right hand a gnarled brown staff
    Made from dead wizard-haunted trees;
    With it thou castest sorceries
—Necromantic powers I quaff

Thy ebony hair, like serpents
    Flows languidly in the night-wind;
    Thy soft long fingers are now twined
In mine, who singeth dread laments.

Thy funereal gown rippleth
    In the howling wind, and damned ghouls
    That lust over Hell's red jewels
Watchest, with glee, my brewing death.

Thy breasts a sorcerer's desire:
    Pale hills laurelled with pink towers
    Salted with tears, and whose powers
Burn the thirsty into hell-fire.

Thine eyes blue pools into Faery
    That I gaze into: undead forms
    That ride on Hell's gigantic worms
Prepare to storm a doomed city.

In thine eyes I discern myself,
    A rotten, desolate, dead husk
    Picked by hungry buzzards at dusk,
As mine health now becomes *thy* health.

Deacon Mercer

Jonathan Thomas

A backwoods ballad of Appalachian Icelanders.

Deacon Mercer did allow
Having almost all he should,
Little missing from his life
Except a wife and fatherhood.

Mercer rode from his estate,
Spurred his horse across the stream,
Till he came to the farm on which
Dwelt the beauty of his dreams.

He called her from the fireside
To stand upon the frozen ground,
He wanted Sara to agree
To spend that Christmas in the town.

He offered her a life of ease,
Nevermore a lowly hired hand.
They whiled the time away with talk
Till dusk lay heavy on the land.

He promised to return on Christmas,
Rode away with heart ablaze,
And when he came to the water's edge
He never saw the icy glaze.

Horse and rider took a headlong
Dive into the riverbed,
Numbing current pulled them under
Soon the deacon would be dead.

Far too sweet had life become
For him to go beneath the sod,
So Deacon Mercer prayed a prayer
Improper to the ears of God.

He crossed the water as a corpse,
They found him by the riverside,
Current now too hard and cold
For news to pass that he had died.

Snow came down on Christmas day,
Clouds hung thick on Christmas night.
Sara heard one knock on the door,
The deacon stood beyond the light.

He had the one horse for them both
And not a single word to say,
Even at the edge of town
When they rode off the other way.

They sped to the river and across,
On ice that should have been too thin.
She saw the graveyard up ahead;
His hat went flying in the wind.

Moonlight burst between the clouds,
And on the back of Mercer's head
Sara saw the white of his skull
In the gash from which his life had bled.

A grave lay open in the graveyard.
"Here's a house for the two of us,"
So he said as he caught her sleeve
And grinned at her with a sickening lust.

The deacon pulled, got Sara's coat,
And stumbled back into the pit.
She ran over to the chapel,
Rang the bell till her ears would split.

With every ring the specter weakened,
Powerless inside the ground,
Till the people who were nearest
Came to see about the sound.

Mercer's grave they filled again
And soon they set a boulder there.
Sara kept on moving west,
But she never married anywhere.

Alastor

Wade German

There is a spirit wandering through space
Of regions most remote and desolate;
That bound to solitudes, may never sate
An impetus to travel place to place—
From boreal wilderness and weird white wastes
To desert dunes that whisper of despair,
It roams eternally the haunted air
Of ruins and lost realms by time effaced.

The spirit but a sourceless shadow seems
Amid mirages on the sighing sands—
Flitting to caves and dark colossal tombs,
Searching for some unknown among those glooms
And silences that speak of other lands,
Of alien worlds that ancient dead men dream.

Weird Tale

Charles Lovecraft

(Dedicated to *The Unique Magazine*)

Grey fumes of weirdness coil about the font
And statues of dark jade. The agate piers
Holding the roof seem like long snakes whose spoors
Have wriggled there by fitful accident,
Or fright. There flops a giant centipede,
And worshippers gyrate their cowled, dark bulks.
There glare down through the fumes the awful hulks
Of vile pre-human gods whose thirsts are freed.

The altar stone aligns with ceiling pores;
A moonbeam burns down through the air aslant;
Strange, croaking voices howl in awful cant
As bestial hands are gnarled with ancient sores;
The victim bound with thongs of skin writhes there;
A devil priest, his mask dislodges *fear*.

Among the Gargoyles

K. A. Opperman

I have seen what these gargoyles have gazed on
From their perilous perches of stone;
I have known what it is to grow crazed on
The mauve mist and the moonlight alone;
And high loneliness, too, I have known.

I have met the mad stare of Polaris
With white eyes just as cold and as hard;
On this ancient cathedral of Paris,
Most grotesque, I am ever its guard,
A mere ghoul irreversibly marred.

I have watched from the shadows as women
In white gowns have considered the ledge . . .
I have felt heart and soul start to dimmen
As, averting my visage, I pledge
Not to startle them over the edge.

In my dreams to the moon I have traveled,
On such wings as not waken by day—
But the vision is ever unraveled
By these gargoyles, these lords of dismay,
Whose gray wings are but anchors to stay.

The Girl with Pennies on Her Eyes

Scott Thomas

Her eyes an autumn sunset sky
Her dress a steam of milk
Less solid, say, than silk
Her gaze a sunset in disguise
Twin shields to guard the tears inside
I wonder how the poor thing died
That girl with pennies on her eyes

The Reunited

Oliver Smith

Mourning for my love, the bright summer days have grown too long
And are curdled with a bitter dust, the street-girls happy laughter
Turned mocking in my rage. I hate the scent of honeysuckle,
Of orange groves, of freshly gathered hay.

I thought I saw her, *my dead love,*
Crawl on her fingertips over the moonlight lawn
arisen from her bed in halls of unfleshed bones
And slipping moth-pale through my window.
My dead love came in
Creeping on her white spider-fingers,
Delicacies and niceties drawing her
Tempting her, inclining her
To inch on a soft white belly.
So slowly she came in
Across the common sallow stone
And marble veined with azure,
Across the threshold of our chamber
where I cried "welcome"
I issued my invitation, sable edged and skulled,
To cloth herself again in our ravaged bed
Bound in scarlet sheets of sin.

Her black tongue whispered in my ear
She shared the secrets of worm,
And rat, and midnight crow

And hummed a strange song,
That, the devil knows how,
Escaped the inquisitorial fires,
And passed unchanged from
The days before sulphur rained
To cleanse the flesh pots of Gomorrah.

Her face sometimes grew kind in candlelight,
Then with shadows bathed
Became more sultry in the midnight heat,
Hungry and vulpine, and at last ardent
As the *one star awake* hid in the glimmer
Of her eyes. She opened her ripe lips,
Unearthly nectar glistening with opiate-sweetness
On their cherry-red swell,
And her kisses grew sharp and cruel with passion.
"Come," she said
And I drank deep of the incarnadine feast
She held within her mouth.

Now my dream lingers, among briars grown
With the reddest rose, with the sharpest thorn
Or like an angel floats above
The flowering hedge rows and silent lakes
Her feet too precious, too holy

To touch the sullen earth
Until day returns her
to the cold rooted-knotted clay
In the first gleam of the hateful sun.

I noticed this morning some transparency in my reflection,
My face a fresh stain upon the marble of an ancient tomb.
No more awake in daylight, but let me burrow
Back beneath deep-moulded leaves and soft black soil,
Returned to timeless vaults
With my dead love in my arms again to sleep,
Wrapped in ancient tapestry, tied by threads
Of faded memory, by dust, by the dregs of life
Drunk from broken cups of mortal flesh,
And let us sleep the day long awaiting the feast
That lies spread in mausoleum, graveyard, and crypt
Across those happy lands among
The ones who live west of the sunset hour.

Graveyard Circumspect

Alan Gullette

At first position, the gravestone
    Casts a cold shadow on me
On my lonely apogee
    Away from the lighthouse.

At second position, my shadow
    Is cast over the graves—
And I stand brave, with
    The lighthouse over my shoulder.

At third position, no shadow is cast—
    As I ride the beam of light
And soar in shamanic flight
    Above the graveyard vast.

At null position, we arrive
    At the extra-centric view,
Where no point takes vantage
    Over other points or views.

The lighthouse has a purpose, all can see.
But the graveyard has no point at all.

Fog of War

Christina Sng

The world is shrouded in fog,
The haze chafing our lungs
With glass-edged soot.

From the horizon
They appear as shadows,
Looming like cloud dragons

We imagined as children,
Passing through towns,
Disintegrating everything.

There is no choice but to
Launch the arks, untested
As they are, into the dark.

The first three explode;
Fireworks in the opaque sky.
But five make it safely

Past our atmosphere
And into the dead zone;
The fathomless vacuum.

The survivors watch in horror
As the cloud dragons devour
What remains:

All our loved ones
Who did not qualify
To fly,

And the hallmarks
Of our beautiful planet:
Our proud trees,

Lush green meadows,
Our grand mountains
And great lakes,

Now a vast nothingness.
Not even a desert.
They even drained the seas dry,

Leaving a empty bowl
Where life used to teem.
Now a metaphor for everything.

Our planet
A lifeless husk
For what could have been.

When the dragons are finally done,
They reach skyward, toward us.
But the vacuum suffocates them,

Turning the fog into frost,
Imploding each cloud
Into the same nothingness

It brought to our world.

Two Fates

John Mundy

I remember the orange moon,
Steel flashing in the cold light,
You clutching the long scarf tightly, honorably
(It was yellow but white in the moonlight),
Neither of us faltering
Or loosening our grip,
The white ribbon clenched in our teeth
As we danced with the fires
Of liquor and madness
And never questioned our Fate;
I no longer remember why—
Perhaps a fleeting Romany girl
Or a drunken hand of cards,
Perhaps the foolish hunger of youth
To taste Life by tasting Death.
It hardly matters now.
You struck the mortal blow,
A fine and honorable kill.

The next morning they hung you
From a twisted tree outside our village.
I would surely have protested
if I were in that mindless crowd;
I died gloriously
And you died like a dog.
Life is sometimes unfair that way.

Alchemy

Ian Futter

No ear to hear
the burgeoning blasts
of vast star-engines
waning fast.

No skin to feel
the waking heat
of burning light
from dark, complete.

No scratch, or wound,
to unmade flesh,
as cooling ash
and rocks enmesh.

No feet to flex
on forming ground,
or hands to wave away
strange sounds

that sing the sun
and moon to place.
No need to cower
in empty space.

No eyes to see
the fading thrones:
Corporeal dogs
chase all gods home.

No mind to know
that all is well;
bare heavens have
no need of hell.

No brow to bow
or heart to yield
on carbon-strewn
Elysian Field.

No breath,
but poisoned breath of stars,
like cankered lungs
ejecting scars.

But there:
A fleck, 'midst maelstrom's host,
extracts itself
from Bedlam's boast.

Werewolf

K. A. Opperman

    The full moon is rising
        From out the red trees,
    Dead branches disguising
        Its leprous disease;
    The Wolf is now rising
        Within, realizing
    My curse, my disease,
This mournful, accursed autumn night.

    I howl to my brothers—
        Wolves answer my call;
    Town maidens and mothers
        Pray Rosary, all.
    The townsmen, my brothers
        By day, are now Others—
    Amassing, they all
Hold pitchforks and torches alight.

    I prowl through the woodland
        Outside of the town—
    A ghoulish, ungood land
        Where wan flowers drown.
    Dark mere of the woodland,
        O what visage should land
    Here?—would it would drown!—
A wolf-face of crimson-eyed fright!

    I tear though their torches,
        Their pitchforks I snap!
    Slay men on their porches,
        Their bright blood to lap!
    A fallen torch torches
        A house, the town scorches!
    Her blood I would lap—
That maiden all moonlight-bedight!

    I sweep up the maiden
        With one savage arm,
    An angel of Aidenn
        Who screams in alarm.
    I kidnap the maiden,
        My claws sweetly laden—
    The bell sounds alarm!
I carry her off, out of sight.

    I fly through the forest,
        The tolling grows far.
    I head for the hoarest
        Of hills, for a Star
    Rules over the forest,
        This night of my sorest
    Of trials! and the Star
Can challenge the moon's awful might.

    Surrounded by roses
        That ruins entwine,
  She sleeps in sprawled poses—
        I see her for mine!
  This lily mid roses,
        Whom tomb-top reposes—
  She *always* was mine!
I lust her white beauty to bite . . .

    The moon becomes veiled
        By curtains of cloud;
  The Star has not failed,
        So silvery proud!
  The Man, lately veiled
        By evil, ungaoled,
  I weep here, unproud,
Above my beloved's cold wight.

    Her white eyelids waken
        Beneath the Star's rays!
  My Faith has been shaken—
        Now seraphs I praise!
  But though she awaken,
        Forever forsaken,
  I sing my sad praise,
Her love nevermore to requite.

Panos

Fred Phillips

Underneath a leafy shelter
Where I sat one quiet day,
Fugitive from summer's swelter,
Holding ennui at bay,

From behind a lofty giant
Stepped a creature into view;
Now although my mind is pliant,
I despair of telling you.

Brown its goat's-legs were, and curly,
Tiny horns atop its crown;
It had risen bright and early
From its pipes to coax a tone.

O! the Christian tale must wither
As we now turn back the clock;
For the creature lingers hither,
Their philosophy to mock.

Dead leaves glorified its haunches;
Its brown eyes were bright as dew,
And it said between the branches,
"Where were you when I needed you?"

Water Tears

Mary Krawczak Wilson

Once I saw an endless shoreline
Where rocks and shells and bones lay dead;
The water wielded its sword—bloody and red,
Leaving no trace of land, nor trees, nor vine.

Once I stood alone on a black-sand beach;
An azure blue eye beamed from a lighthouse,
Cyclops signaling its last breath; now posthumous
Dim, dark, and dying—immortality never to be reached.

Once I sailed into the infinite ocean;
The froth, form, and fury of the waves
Roiled and raged—leaving a wake of watery graves
Where lives were lost not now, but when?

Once I succumbed to the call of the sea,
A void where once appeared the sun, the earth, and the moon:
Alive am I—only to drown in unfathomable depths too soon.
Is it true: In death, the soul is eternal and the body is freed?

The Summons

David Barker

On wind-swept nights
do spirits linger,
extending forth
a decayed finger?

To prod the living
from their slumber,
a call to join
their spectral number?

Teeming at the
ancient gates,
to burst the bolts
where Death awaits?

Emissaries from
the ebon tomb,
dragging souls
to eternal doom?

This I ask on
gust-chilled eves,
when something stirs
midst rotted leaves.

The Witching Hour

Alicia Cole

onion loam, and grandmother
spinning: lanterns light
    the dead of night

when only the moon coughs
and rattles, a pale sliver
    of black cat bone

Classic Reprints

St. Irvyne's Tower

Percy Bysshe Shelley

How swiftly through Heaven's wide expanse
    Bright day's resplendent colours fade!
How sweetly does the moonbeam's glance
    With silver tint St. Irvyne's glade!

No cloud along the spangled air
    Is borne upon the evening breeze;
How solemn is the scene! how fair
    The moonbeams rest upon the trees!

Yon dark gray turret glimmers white,
    Upon it sits the mournful owl;
Along the stillness of the night
    Her melancholy shriekings roll.

But not alone on Irvyne's tower
    The silver moonbeam pours her ray;
It gleams upon the ivied bower,
    It dances in the cascade's spray.

"Ah! why do dark'ning shades conceal
    The hour, when man must cease to be?
Why may not human minds unveil
    The dim mists of futurity?

"The keenness of the world hath torn
    The heart which opens to its blast;
Despised, neglected, and forlorn,
    Sinks the wretch in death at last."

[First published in Shelley's novel *St. Irvyne; or, The Rosicrucian* (London: J. J. Stockdale, 1811).]

His Dream

W. B. Yeats

I swayed upon the gaudy stern
The butt-end of a steering-oar,
And saw wherever I could turn
A crowd upon the shore.

And though I would have hushed the crowd,
There was no mother's son but said,
"What is the figure in a shroud
Upon a gaudy bed?"

And after running at the brim
Cried out upon that thing beneath
—It had such dignity of limb—
By the sweet name of Death.

Though I'd my finger on my lip,
What could I but take up the song?
And running crowd and gaudy ship
Cried out the whole night long.

Crying amid the glittering sea,
Naming it with ecstatic breath,
Because it had such dignity,
By the sweet name of Death.

[First published in Yeats's *The Green Helmet and Other Poems* (Churchtown, Ireland: Cuala Press, 1910).]

Cthulhu

David E. Schultz

Beneath the waves, locked in his massive crypt,
Dead Cthulhu stumbles on his slimy claws,
Sealed mercifully from man by cosmic laws
Where, since Time's birth, a star-born ooze has dripped.
Lumb'ring along the fearsome avenues
Of the corpse-city, 'mong the wailing dead,
As nightmares fill the writhing dragonhead
And slowly to his worshippers diffuse.
Vast solar systems pivot toward the scheme
That frees the Great Old Ones from living death
To mount the titan blocks to R'lyeh's gate
And taint our tiny earth with their foul breath.
I wake in horror from this repellent dream
And vainly curse the stars that liberate.

[First published in *Nyctalops* 2, No. 3 (January–February 1975): 37.]

Articles

The Poets of *Weird Tales*: Part 1

Frank Coffman

When two poems appeared in the fifth issue of *Weird Tales* (July–August 1923), a publication dubbed as "The Unique Magazine," a tradition of including verse in its pulp pages was begun. Significantly, perhaps prophetically, those two poems, "The Garden of Evil" and "The Red Moon," were the work of Clark Ashton Smith, who would become one of the three poets most frequently published in the magazine's famous first run (1923-54).

The other two members of this elite group were Smith's fellows in what most critics of pulp fiction see as *Weird Tales*'s "Great Triumvirate" of author-poets: Howard Phillips Lovecraft and Robert Ervin Howard. According to the poems listed in Jaffery and Cook's *The Collector's Index to* Weird Tales,[1] Smith would eventually have thirty-nine of his poems published in the magazine, including one under the pseudonym of "Timeus Gaylord" (his father's first name and his mother's maiden name). Lovecraft attained the total of forty-three, including most of his *Fungi from Yuggoth* sonnet sequence. Howard would have thirty-five.

While later incarnations of *Weird Tales* after the first series have also included verse, most of the poems in later runs of the magazine were reprints of earlier poems. After that first run of little more than three decades, ending in 1954, very little verse appeared in "The Unique Magazine." The present discussion will focus on the poets and poetry of that first, classic set of volumes of the pulp era.

The verses published in *Weird Tales* range in quality from lumps of

---

1. Sheldon Jaffery and Fred Cook, *The Collector's Index to* Weird Tales (Bowling Green, OH: Bowling Green State University Popular Press, 1985), 128-42.

coal to diamonds of great value, and there are some that shine like stars, exemplifying artistry and poetic virtuosity. Many of these, of course, are from the justly recognized pens of the triumvirs, but many are from writers whose overall achievements—especially in verse—have been vastly undervalued, including some definite gems from lesser (or at least less acclaimed and noted) contributors.

Smith, after all, actually took the prize for number of contributions, since he was the translator of all eight of the poems by Charles P. Baudelaire that were to appear in the magazine (including one as translated by "Timeus Gaylord") and another translation of a poem by Paul Verlaine (also with "Timeus Gaylord" as translator). It should be noted that there are some few discrepancies regarding the number of successful submissions by the three triumvirs. Stephen Jones[2] compiles only forty-one poems for Lovecraft, but thirty-seven for Howard in his important *The Complete Poems from* Weird Tales series, which devotes a book to each of the three.

In terms of prolific output, several other versifiers of varying degrees of skill contributed mightily to that first incarnation of the pulp. Dorothy Quick and Leah Bodine Drake—the two most frequently published women in the early run—each had success with twenty-four of their submissions. These two were followed, in terms of what we might at least call "numerical success," by four poets of the early years: A. Leslie (pseudonym for Alexander Leslie Scott, the writer of many successful western and adventure stories and novels) contributed twenty-three poems by 1935; Cristel Hastings, eighteen by 1938; Edgar Daniel Kramer, seventeen by 1937; and Donald Wandrei (also, of course, one of the most prolific short story contributors to *Weird Tales*), seventeen by 1932.

After these four, we have, in descending order of number of poems published (but having at least five): Frank Belknap Long Jr., close friend of Lovecraft (12); Alfred I. Tooke (12); Clarence Edwin Flynn (9); Page Cooper (full name: Anise Page Cooper; however, all her contributions

---

2. Robert E. Howard, *The Singer in the Mist and* Others (Hornsea, UK: Stanza Press, 2010); H. P. Lovecraft, *Halloween in a Suburb and Others* (Hornsea, UK: Stanza Press, 2010); Clark Ashton Smith, *Song of the Necromancer and Others* (Hornsea, UK: Stanza Press, 2010); all edited by Stephen Jones.

are from the 1940s and '50s) (8); Harriet Bradfield (6); Stanton A. Coblentz, reviewer, critic, and science fiction writer (6); Mary Elizabeth Counselman, author of the classic and wildly popular *Weird Tales* story "The Three Marked Pennies" (6); Marion Doyle (6); Yetza Gillespie (5); Francis Hard (pseudonym for *Weird Tales* editor Farnsworth Wright!) (5); Edith Hurley (5); Alice l'Anson (5); Robert Nelson, a brilliant poetic voice who died young, a day before his twenty-third birthday (5); and Hung Long Tom, the more curious (and salacious) of the pseudonyms of Frank Owen (5).

There are also several single poems of significance, some "one-hit wonders," which find their way into the pages of *Weird Tales*: Robert H. Barlow's tributary poem following the death of Robert E. Howard (October 1936); Percy Bysshe Shelley's immortal "Ozymandias," perhaps the most efficient narrative sonnet in the language, inclusive of three narrative voices and a frame story in fourteen lines; and one by George Sterling (November 1928), whose person and whose poetry had great influence upon Clark Ashton Smith (and, by extension through Smith, Donald Wandrei), Jack London, and Robinson Jeffers. Sterling's early and seminal poem, "A Wine of Wizardry," became the standard for early twentieth-century romantic and imaginative poetry, flying in the face of the rise of both realism and free verse, causing much controversy and critical discussion.

Topics, Themes, and Forms

Though the "weird," as declared in the magazine's name, begs for the typical contributions to be in the realm of the supernatural, exotic, and the overall motif of the "unbelievable-but-true," the topics covered in *Weird Tales* are by no means all in that vein. Several poems were dedicated to authors and poets who had contributed to the magazine and had come to untimely ends. There are tributes and commemoratives to Howard and to Poe, and four to Lovecraft—these last including poems by Henry Kuttner, Frank Belknap Long Jr., and Clark Ashton Smith.

Thematically, the poems range across all the subgenres of the horrific and supernatural: ghosts and ghostly occurrences of various types; witchcraft, demonic possessions and the occult; monstrous creatures, including werewolves, vampires, ghouls, revenants and zombies, etc.; reincarnation; and some that fall simply under what Lovecraft would call, in the introduction to his important "Supernatural Horror in Literature," "the weird tale."[3] Curiously, some of the poetry touches upon science fictional themes and topics from the era when many were still calling it by Hugo Gernsback's term, "scientifiction," or even "skiffy." At least one poem by Vincent Starrett—poet of the famous Sherlockian tributary sonnet, "221B"—"Dupin and Another" (August 1939), clearly verges into the detection and mystery realm. Poems of transience and impermanence, and a few touching upon remembrance of the Great War are also to be found. Several of Clark Ashton Smith's inclusions are best understood as romantic lyrics professing love. One of the best illustrations of the wide-ranging scope of Weird Tales poetic themes is Francis Hard's poem "After Two Nights of the Ear-Ache":

> Most gentle Sleep! Two nights I wooed in vain;
> Thou wouldst not come to banish racking pain:
> For what is Sleep but Life in stone bound fast?
> Oblivion of the Present, Future, Past.

It is likely that Wright could decide upon the inclusion of that "masterpiece" himself, although the bar to hurdle for successful publication in "The Unique Magazine" was often not set very high—for fiction as well as for verse. A magazine, after all, has to make sure it survives before it can thrive—and that means copy to publish, pages to fill.

As to form, the poetry of Weird Tales is almost entirely traditional rhymed and metered verse. While *vers libre* was already in vogue among the more "progressive" poetic publications and the circles of the literati, almost the entirety of the poetry to find its way onto the pulp pages of Weird Tales was traditional verse in traditional and often fixed verse forms. This is clearly in keeping with an anti-modernist literary perspective and even a reaffirmation of the early Gothic and the later supernatural traditions of the nineteenth century.

In keeping with the proportions of Western and European tradition since the early Italian Renaissance, the most common type of poem is

---

3. H. P. Lovecraft, *The Annotated Supernatural Horror in Literature*, ed. S. T. Joshi (New York: Hippocampus Press, 2nd ed. 2012), 28.

the sonnet—but in a plethora of experimental and variant as well as traditional forms. What is different about many of the sonnets in *Weird Tales* is the use of the "fourteener" as a vehicle of *narrative* rather than its traditional *lyric* content. The "Story Sonnet" finds a decided niche in the magazine. These micro-narratives, attempting to compress a tale into the small square of poetry that the *quatorzain* demands, are frequently unsuccessful—but when they work to achieve the desired effect upon the reader, as Poe advocated in his important essay upon Hawthorne's *Twice-Told Tales*,[4] the impact of such concision is remarkable. Some of the fine examples are found in poems by our triumvirate to be discussed below.

As to the types of sonnets, the traditional Italian or Petrarchan form is found (in the classic *abbaabba* octave and in both the common sestets: *cdcdcd* and *cdecde* with a few variant sestets, but in keeping with the rule forbidding a couplet ending); several of the sonnets follow Thomas Wyatt's early English variation (known, appropriately, as "Wyatt's Sonnet," also used by John Donne and others, rhyming *abbaabba cddcee*); several are in the English or Shakespearean mode (*abab cdcd efef gg*); there are plenty of experimental "blends" of the Italian and English (as is the case with most of Lovecraft's *Fungi from Yuggoth* poems); and there are other experiments and oddities, including the rare classic Sicilian form (*abababab cdcdcd*).

After the sonnet forms, including any and all fourteen-line poems, come the varieties of the ballad—both mock "folk" and "literary," the former following the *abcb* rhyme scheme with lines of 4343 accents and several examples of the stanza cadences of both the "long ballad" (4444 accents) and the "short ballad" (3343 or 3333 accents). The modern literary forms of the ballad make greater use of regularized iambic metrics and occasionally the *abab* rhyme pattern.

---

4. Edgar Allan Poe, "Review of *Twice-Told Tales* By Nathaniel Hawthorne," *Graham's Magazine* (May 1842) 298-99. ("the unity of effect or impression is a point of the greatest importance . . . having conceived, with deliberate care, a certain unique or single effect to be wrought out, he then invents such incidents—he then combines such events as may best aid him in establishing this preconceived effect.")

Most commonly, after the sonnet and ballad forms and varieties are poems in quatrain stanzas, including the iambic pentameter "heroic quatrain" (*abab*), the couplet quatrain (*aabb*), and even examples using the rubaiyat quatrain (*aaba*). Many of the longer poems display a wide variety of stanza patterns, meters, and rhyming patterns. It must also be noted that many of the "verses," as they were called in the indices to *Weird Tales*, are tiny poems of a single quatrain or poems of only 8 to 12 lines. Many of the poems were, as with the prose fiction, accompanied by illustrations from various *Weird Tales* artists—most notably several by Virgil Finlay. There are almost no examples of free verse to be found. There are some examples of the very restrictive "fixed forms": villanelle, rondel, rondeau, and the like.

All in all, the vast majority of the forms displayed in the first run of *Weird Tales* conform to the rules and standards of traditional and conventional rhymed verse. As might well be expected, variations of the two most ubiquitous patterns in Western literature, the sonnet and the ballad, are most prevalent.

Reviews

In the Court of Hades

Adam Bolivar

K. A. OPPERMAN. *The Crimson Tome*. Preface by Dr. W. C. Farmer. Introduction by Donald Sidney-Fryer. New York: Hippocampus Press, 2015. 182 pp. $15.00 tpb.

Let me say right out of the gate how impressed I am with the virtuosity on display in K. A. Opperman's debut poetry collection, *The Crimson Tome*. Some of the poems in this book must surely rank among the very finest I have ever read. Opperman's confident mastery of complex forms of rhyme and meter makes the end result look easy, but as a fellow practitioner of the craft I can assure you that it is not. There is as much sweat on these pages as there are crimson drops of blood.

Not content with the conventional fourteen-line Shakespearean sonnet cleaved to by less resourceful poets, Opperman strikes out and invents his own fifteen-line sonnet, with its own unique rhyme structure, which he wields as a master swordsman his custom-forged blade. Each of these "Oppermanian" sonnets is divided into two sections, following in the Petrarchan tradition: an octet to establish the proposition and a septet to initiate a change in thought and arrive at a resolution.

> There is an ancient, isolated town
> Hemmed in by hills and woodlands without end,
> Where autumn's crimson wound will never mend,
> And jack-o'-lanterns all year long grin down
> From crooked fence and sagging porch, to ward
> Against the woodland wraiths that nightly wend
> Along those roads that ghostly fog would drown,
> With witch-light eyes that weigh each goblin gourd. . . .
>
> A sleepiness pervades there like a spell,

> And all are lost who find that haunting place—
> For none have come there of their own accord,
> And none may leave who in that country dwell.
> Some lurking necromancy seems to lace
> Yorehaven's very air—enough to quell
> The strongest will to leave her strange embrace.

And not just sonnets: alexandrines, innovative experiments in metrical variation, even a ballad or two can be found in *The Crimson Tome*, whose pages lay out a varied and sumptuous feast of poetic styles for the reader's delectation. One of my favorites, in fact, is a metrically rather simple ballad done with pulpish "sword-and-sorcery" flair, "Duel with the Dark Double," which describes a clash between a crimson-cloaked hero and his daemonic doppelgänger. The simple heartbeat rhythm of the poem works perfectly to evoke the visceral excitement of the action.

> From out the moonshade of a tree,
>   My doppelgänger stepped:
> A phantom black as death was he,
>   And on my path he kept.
>
> I drew my sword, its argent glowed,
>   Surcharged by aegis moon;
> He drew his shadow-sword, and showed
>   He meant to battle soon.
>
> He waited there, a sentinel
>   Upon the forking path:
> As if by sympathetic spell,
>   I shared his cunning wrath.
>
> I started with a fell attack,
>   To seek an instant kill—
> But lunar silver clashed with black,
>   And rang with thwarted will.

Who says poetry need be dull? That, I think, is the crux of Opperman's achievement—that he is not some mere "meter monkey" showing off his mechanical cleverness. He is able to summon real moods and vivid visual imagery and dazzle with fantastic wordplay and vocabulary while simultaneously composing seamless meter that sounds perfectly natural when read aloud. There are few others who could rival this achievement, and that is what makes it hen's-tooth rare. Although K. A. Opperman insists that his primary influence is Clark Ashton Smith (to whom, as a fellow Californian, he is a worthy heir as a weird poet), the only other I can think of who employed such a wide array of poetic forms is that great Bostonian, Edgar Allan Poe. And like Poe, Opperman treats a poem as an engineering problem rather than a flight of whimsy: a bridge of words to be scrupulously architected and deployed. To all who doubt this methodology, I say only: observe the result.

> Grimoire and volumen, stone tablet, tome,
> Line endless shelves, in archives veiled with Night—
> Retrieveless, save by skeleton and wight,
> Which down those aisles in silence deathward roam.
> It is the doom of words to molder there—
> No text immortal is to sateless Time.
> Mayhap some wraith will read my dusty rhyme
> While stumbling down oblivion's ebon stair.

I would be remiss if I did not pause to admire the gorgeous illustrations capably furnished by Steve Lines. His surreal and sometimes erotic images capture the tone that pervades *The Crimson Tome*—a strange blend of the gruesome and the sensual.

My only cavil with this collection would be its overreliance on a few hoary themes—vampires, succubi, moonlit graveyards, jack-o'-lanterns . . . at least half a dozen poems about Hallowe'en—all the usual suspects of Gothic cliché. This is not to say that originality is nowhere to be found. The sonnet cycle that opens the book follows a Randolph Carter-like dreamer's travels through the "Land of Darkest Dreams" in search of the titular Crimson Tome. His dream-quest takes him to a quaint and curious town called Yorehaven, a name that any fantasist would be pleased to conjure. And near the close of the book, Opperman invokes eleventh-century Persian poet Omar Khayyám (author of that exquisite paean to decadence, the *Rubiáyát*) and ventures into territory that I found particularly refreshing.

> Where is the wine Khayyam would have me quaff?
> What sanguine grape will gush forth juice enough?
>   And from what gilded cup, pray, should I sip?—
> My dromedary I must soon fall off. . . .
>
> Long have I traveled with this caravan,
> Forsaking all the pleasures of Ispahan,
>   But in no far-flung land have found to drip
> The precious Vintage, since my quest began.
>
> Omar Khayyam, have you no little wine
> Yet left within your jug—that modest shrine
>   For such a grand elixir?—Have you no
> Single drop left that I, parched, might make mine?

    I would adjure the poet in his future efforts, while not abandoning the Gothic conceits so central to his vision, perhaps also to explore some less trodden realms of the fantastique to see what strange jewels he may find glittering in the bramble.

    Before I conclude, I must also give due praise to the "Ashiel" cycle at the heart (both literally and figuratively) of the book. These poems, which are amatory offerings to the poet's beloved, Ashley Dioses (a formidable poet in her own right), reveal Opperman at his most vulnerable and most romantic . . .

> No sorceress has ever cast
> A stronger spell
> Than that placed on me three moons past
>   By Ashiel.
>
> In misty moonlit garths where grows
> The asphodel
> Of poison purple, and the rose
>   As red as hell,

> She worked her witch's charms on me,
> > Worked them so well;
> Bedrugged by perfume, sleepily,
> > For her I fell.

I look forward to see where the *pas-de-deux* of these talented poets will take them in years to come—perhaps to the very court of Hades, whom Mr. Opperman may enchant with his exquisite verses no less than Orpheus himself. He has surely beguiled me.

Enlightenment from the Outer Dark

Donald Sidney-Fryer

WADE GERMAN. *Dreams from a Black Nebula*. New York: Hippocampus Press, 2014. 134 pp. $15.00 tpb.

In case no one else in a regular print medium has expressed or emphasized it—unless a reviewer or a poet has done so in the three issues of *Spectral Realms* to date (magisterially edited by S. T. Joshi) and I have overlooked it—the genre of imaginative poetry (the poetry of fantasy and science fiction, if you prefer) has been undergoing not just a renaissance but a super-efflorescence as well, at least some time since the first decade of the twenty-first century, with the founding and flourishing of Hippocampus Press under the astute guidance of owner-editor Derrick Hussey and his *vezir* S. T. Joshi. The word *assistant* or even *colleague* cannot do justice to the creative role played by Joshi not only concerning Hippocampus Press but just as much concerning the modern field of imaginative literature in general and poetry in particular. Both Hussey and Joshi have great learning and cultivation in regard to the arts (and not just the art of literature), to the benefit of all concerned.

    I realize that I open myself to the charge of logrolling in praising either one or both of Messrs. Hussey and Joshi, because I have engaged with them professionally, and I have benefited from that. However, I merely state the obvious truth. No other publisher in the genre of fantasy and science fiction makes available so much new poetry, moreover in traditional form (and of polished craftsmanship), as does Hippocampus Press. Although I am gratefully aware of this contemporary cornucopia, I cannot keep up with it, however deserving of praise and meritorious in itself it may be. I simply remain astounded and mute with admiration, sitting on the sidelines.

Messrs. Hussey and Joshi seem to have set themselves as a main goal of Hippocampus Press the publication and promulgation of prose and poetry by Lovecraft, Clark Ashton Smith, and other members of the Old Guard, plus the works of meritorious contemporary authors and poets, some of whom happen to perpetuate certain aspects of the work by the Old Guard. I do know some of these people and their writings, because they appear alongside mine in *Spectral Realms*. Sometimes I do get to know some of it in depth, an occasional volume or two, as in the present case.

Early in the spring of 2015 I received from Derrick Hussey a copy of *Dreams from a Black Nebula,* by Wade German, of which volume I remain the grateful recipient. I looked it over and realized at once that Mr. German, a poet of considerable talent, had expended a great amount of care and craftsmanship on the poems included in this not so slender book, elegantly laid out and printed, of 134 pages. Single short poems have each their own page!—*comme il faut.*

German has obviously mastered meter and rhyme as exemplified in such demanding forms as the sonnet, the sestina, the quatrain, the pantoum, the triolet, and so forth. He knows how to lay out an idea, an image, a concept, and then develop it accordingly. He has also mastered his own version of free verse and free form, but in as disciplined and impeccable a manner as that displayed in the traditional forms. Contrary to received opinion or uninformed expectation, to do good work in free verse demands almost as much dedication and skill as in the received forms.

Like many poets of the weird and supernatural, German continues certain aspects and nuances in verse pioneered by Lovecraft, George Sterling, Ashton Smith, and those in prose by E. A. Poe, Robert W. Chambers, and Jack Vance. More strategically, the poetry that German mines most of all, and most importantly, belongs to himself. Despite his apparently close reading of Lovecraft's great modern sequence, *Fungi from Yuggoth,* not to mention much of Ashton Smith's impressive corpus of poetry, German draws upon his own inventive and versatile imagination, thus fulfilling the one chief desideratum that Baudelaire himself rightfully insisted should inhere in poetry: imagination, or (in French) *l'imaginaire.*

Rather than pontificate in some highfalutin' fashion on German's poetics—a task not to my taste, and for which I have little formal aptitude—let me describe the contents of his volume, and let me quote from the poetry here and there throughout. He devotes as much care to his titles as to the poems themselves, so that the given title thus becomes a supplementary line, a trick, or technique, formidably exploited by poets during the nineteenth century. I need here and now cite (from page 20) title and poem, equally evocative: the "Château Névréant." Just as the sonnet itself seems like a capsule version of "The Dark Château" by Ashton Smith, the title is a neat, lovely play on Malnéant ("A Night in Malnéant"—one of the shortest and most sublime of Smith's shorter prose fictions), which in itself means literally an "ill or evil nothingness," perhaps an aspect of the outer void (the cosmos at large) or of some locale extant in a forgotten corner of France.

Thus, through the agency of Magister German, Malnéant creates a sequel to itself, combining *never* with *ant*, to come forth as "nay-vray-AHNT." One could pronounce Malnéant in the French manner as "mahl-nay-AH^n"—or slightly anglicizing it as "mahl-nay-AHNT." How I would love to read some chronicles—under the heading of the Château Névréant—the narratives of which would ideally serve as a magic sesame to other worlds of beauty, splendor, and the pristine! But let me quote in full the sonnet in question:

> The cypress shadows spread a cryptic gloom
> Across the portal of the old château;
> And statues in the courtyard weirdly loom
> Like watchers on an alien plateau.
> Past crumbling stairs, dark halls and chambers seem
> Too vast and void of solace for repose—
> As if supernal forces had enclosed
> This space in strange dimensions of a dream.
>
> Dark echoes out of time are anchored here.
> The portraits, armor, faded tapestries
> Would speak of baleful crimes and unknown things;
> As if a word might summon to appear
> The presence of a spectral agency
> Still bound by spells in some conjurer's ring.

Like any self-respecting craftsman working in traditional forms, German engineers his lines for maximum effects of sonority, for the ultimate music of the poetic statement itself. He does not permit his native talent or natural facility to betray him into stupidities or gaucheries. He does not fear to use imperfect rhymes or to go against the meter briefly for an occasional foot or so. While his poems read well enough in silence, they sound even better when read or recited out loud, the ultimate test of poetry. Try it, dear reader! Read some of these poems aloud to a sympathetic friend who loves poetry, particularly poems of the fantastic and the supernatural. German skillfully utilizes repetitions in whole or in part to create haunting echoes or echo-like impressions. This dexterity comes into particular or spectacular play in his adroit pantoums—by the very nature of the form itself—some of the best that I have encountered to date. Let me quote one or more typical specimens.

THE NIGHT FOREST
I saw the shadows moving there
Like sentinels among the trees;
They stood like symbols in the air
Of long-forgotten memory.

Like sentinels among the trees,
Arisen from the ancient night
Of long-forgotten memory,
They gathered in the pale moonlight.

Arisen out of ancient night,
As if attendant to old ways,
They gathered in the pale moonlight,
Arisen out of other days.

As if attendant to old ways,
The stood like symbols in the air
Arisen out of other days—
I knew the shadows moving there.

SHADOW AND SILENCE
—After Poe.

A demon spoke to me a rune:
Strange things in time shall be unsealed
Beneath a sky without a moon,
And secret things shall be revealed.

Strange things in time shall be unsealed
Without a shadow of a sound;
And secret things shall be revealed
In silence on a shadowed ground.

Without a shadow of a sound,
An ebon sleep as smooth as glass
Like silence on a shadowed ground
For many centuries shall pass.

An ebon sleep as smooth as glass
Beneath a sky without a moon
For many centuries shall pass.
And thus the demon spoke his rune.

(The last pantoum constitutes not just a beautiful tribute to Poe but specifically to his twin extraordinary poems in prose "Shadow—A Parable" and "Silence—A Fable.")

I must record and commend with a certain astonishment the becoming humility of German as a poetic practitioner vis-à-vis his immediate poetic and prose progenitors, as one who follows in their footsteps, that is, the footsteps of E. A. Poe, A. C. Swinburne, Robert W. Chambers, George Sterling, Ashton Smith, Jack Vance, and Karl Edward Wagner. The Swinburne connection in particular amazes me: few poets today would have the wit, the panache, the skill to learn from, or mimic, the poetry of Swinburne. Although echoing the rhythms and accents of Swinburne for his own purposes, going from Swinburne's diffuseness to his own succinctness, the similarities between Swinburne's "Hendecasyllabics" (38 lines) and those of German's (the exact same title but with 47 lines) are very close indeed, and rather startling. We quote the first eleven lines of both poems to show the subtle transformation effected by German from Swinburne's original. Swinburne comes first, followed at once by German.

> In the month of the long decline of roses,
> I, beholding the summer dead before me,
> Set my face to the sea and journeyed silent,
> Gazing eagerly where above the sea-mark
> Flame as fierce as the fervid eyes of lions
> Half divided the eyelids of the sunset;
> Till I heard as it were a noise of waters
> Moving tremulous under feet of angels
> Multitudinous, out of all the heavens;
> Knew the fluttering wind, the fluttered foliage
> Shaken fitfully, full of sound and shadow;

> In the month of the seventh moon of Saturn,
> I, surveying the landscape spread before me,
> Placed my feet on a path and outward wandered
> Dead dry land in the realm beyond the border,
> Crossing region of rock and giant craters
> Till I reached in the twilight open desert—
> Strange red reaches of dune and desolation
> Endless, emptied of all, without oases,
> Where I saw the mirages merge with shadows,
> Flitting spectrally out among the ruins
> Half submerged in the sand—the ancient temples.

Only a very good and metrically ingenious poet-craftsman could so closely echo the essentially inimitable Swinburne, and use his narrative structure for his own creative purposes and ultimately very different ends!

But perhaps we find the unconditional apex of German's invention as well as technical skill in "The Necromantic Wine," in what ranks as the longest poem in this exceptional collection, in what is as a poetic performance no less impressive than his "Hendecasyllabics."

The two passages quoted as epigraphs at the head of this remarkable effusion announce at once the precise tradition in which our poet continues: "A Wine of Wizardry" by George Sterling and "The Hashish-Eater" by Ashton Smith. Like Sterling's poem "The Necromantic Wine" begins quietly at sunset, as opposed to "The Hashish-Eater," which starts with as magnificent, if not munificent, imperial fanfare as one could imagine. But a quiet beginning can turn out as effective as any imperial summons. Without the potential threat of the dreaded anticlimax, the quiet début comfortably lures the reader into an inviting but potentially dangerous terrain.

Experiencing these visions, the informed reader perceives that German has added to his catalogue or procession of visions (all cast in a supple blank verse) much new lore gleaned from the more recent findings of astronomy and science. In vain would I quote further from this volume or from "The Necromantic Wine" (that is, beyond the title itself), a narrative longer than "A Wine of Wizardry" by a third, and shorter than "The Hashish-Eater" by a half. (The texture of German's poem is much lighter than that of Smith's magnum opus.) All that I can do is to urge prospective readers to acquire this volume, and savor for themselves both the volume and this especial but unpretentious effusion or elucubration. In writing under such direct influence of any pre-existing literary work, in whole or in part, the author faces at once a formidable challenge in order to succeed on his own terms. Can he avoid mere pastiche or, what is worse, unconscious parody? Our poet here succeeds in projecting his own vision, and on his own terms, and creates a worthy congener or companion to the two earlier works, the one by Sterling, the other by Smith.

Re-reading this longer poem for my own intimate perception, and not force-feeding it to myself on behalf of a review, I much enjoy the visions in and of themselves. The premises are admirably stated and cogently developed. The language is always adroit, elegant, and beautiful, with the same artful combination (as exemplified so acutely in Smith, Sir Thomas Browne, Shakespeare, Marlowe, etc.) of Graeco-Latinate polysyllables and Anglo-Saxon of one and/or only several syllables. I would now rank "The Necromantic Wine" almost on the same level as "A Wine of Wizardry," that is, in my own considered or re-considered opinion.

The fantastic or "supernatural" poets of today, those working in traditional forms, have luckily found a format, a market, and a forum for their visions through Hippocampus Press, thanks to the triumvirate of Derrick Hussey, S. T. Joshi, and David E. Schultz (who typesets the material)—just as Ashton Smith as a poet posthumously has discovered his own "school" of poets and his own public following that earlier one of 1912 through 1926 (and somewhat later), that literate public in Northern California that responded to his first four poetry collections, dating to 1912, 1918, 1922, and 1925. In the introduction to his collected *Essays and Introductions* (1961), W. B. Yeats takes it upon himself to "speak the truth," clairvoyantly: "A poet is justified not by the expression of himself, but by the public that he finds or creates; a public ready to his hand if he is a mere popular poet, but a new public, a new form of life, if he is a man of genius." As remarkable as Eliot and Pound proved themselves as innovative poets in the 1920s and afterwards, that is, in the then modern idiom, Yeats here has pronounced the truth about poetry as a species of intuitive magic. Sometimes a great poet-genius does not find his public, his lasting public, immediately; but eventually he does discover it, after touching the lives of many poets, or the select few, of the requisite sensitivity.

A final remark. If the sorcerer who is Wade German speaks the truth in the final line of "The Necromantic Wine"—a sweet reminiscence of Ashton Smith, "This sorcerer departs!"—I sincerely hope that he will still return on occasion, and give us the news from wherever he travels in the great beyond!

Two Centuries of Pleasing Terrors

Steven J. Mariconda

BRETT RUTHERFORD, ed. *Tales of Terror: The Supernatural Poem Since 1800, Volume One*. Providence RI: Poet's Press, 2015. 328 pp. $19.95 tpb.

Tales of Terror is a continuation of a project begun at the end of the eighteenth century by Matthew Gregory Lewis with *Tales of Wonder* (1801). The latter anthology, edited by the notorious author of *The Monk* (1796), proved to be a milestone of Romantic poetry and a bellwether of the Gothic. Lewis did yeoman's work in collecting a wide range of horror ballads, including original and traditional works, adaptations, translations, and even parodies of the Gothic. Sir Walter Scott and Robert Southey contributed supernatural verses, and many important contemporaries, include Shelley (and therefore his successors) fell under strongly its influence.

In 2012, Brett Rutherford's own edition of *Tales of Wonder* (also from Poet's Press) offered reliable texts of the poems, added extensive annotations, and documented the provenance (e.g., folklore) of Lewis's selections. Popular balladry, with its strong basis in local legends, was the emphasis of the first volume; and this collection takes up the thread of that tradition. As such, the material in *Tales of Wonder* and *Tales of Terror* represents the antecedent of modern supernatural fiction. H. P. Lovecraft astutely noted in "Supernatural Horror in Literature" (1927) that it is "genuinely remarkable that weird [prose] narration as a fixed and academically recognized literary form should have been so late of final birth" relative to supernatural poetry.

In his informative introduction to Volume One of *Tales of Terror*, Rutherford notes that the Gothic is by its nature retrospective, and sometimes making it challenging for the contemporary to connect with emotionally. As it puts it, "the poems here are unlikely to frighten . . . [but may] delight those of a Gothic predilection who enjoy the sublime frisson of danger and supernatural awe." The editor's avowed intent is to focus on supernatural themes that are *narrative* in nature rather than "mood pieces, and poems that merely convey atmosphere without incident." It is in this context, then, that the book must be appraised; and it succeeds in both breadth and depth. From a chronological perspective, the volume opens with Joel Barlow (b. 1754) and closes with Fyodor Sologub (b. 1863).

Lovecraft marked the beginning of modern supernatural fiction with Edgar Allan Poe (b. 1809). In poetry, too, the latter marks a convenient dividing line between more traditional themes (e.g., ghosts) and the terror that is "of the soul." A goodly selection of Poe is provided here—in fact, *all* the poems the editor considers to be overtly supernatural. As a pendant, we also get Sarah Helen Whitman's "The Raven" (1848), a valentine to the Master that precipitated their ill-advised romance (see Rutherford's outstanding *Last Flowers: The Romance and Poetry of Edgar Allan Poe and Sarah Helen Whitman* [2011] for more on this and Mrs. Whitman's unexpectedly good poems).

Surprisingly, the sedate Henry Wadsworth Longfellow shines in no fewer than seven items, gaining power from his familiarity with Norse mythology, Native American tradition, and German literature. "Torquemada" (1863) presents the Spanish Inquisition in Gothic trappings of superstition, intolerance, and horror. John Greenleaf Whittier, another staid American normally not associated with excursions into the outré, offers "The Double-Headed Snake of Newbury" (1859), verses based on an incident recorded Cotton Mather.

Along with Poe, Coleridge is a keystone for much of modern supernatural literature—here the deathless *Rime of the Ancient Mariner*, its allegory cast in a calculatedly arcane style. Percy Bysshe Shelley, similarly influential, is represented by multiple original items, as well as a translation of "The Witches' Sabbath" episode from Goethe's *Faust*. Sir Walter Scott, also a titan forebear, is also featured, not merely by stand-alone pieces but also by supernatural poems culled from the novels that stand well on their own.

The editor is to be lauded in renewing several neglected artists. One such is Frances H. Green (1805-1878), Rhode Island reformer and author on abolition, history, and spiritualism. Another is William Bell Scott (1811–1890), a Scottish poet and visual artist. Bell has three powerful poems here, apparently influenced by Rossetti.

The Slavic imagination, vivid with magical beings and spirits, makes a strong showing. There are two excellent poems by Sologub (1863–1927), both concerning the diabolic. Alexander Pushkin's "The Demons," sensitively rendered into English by the editor himself, also provides a real chill. The French probably contribute the most impactful "weirdness" to the volume: Théophile Gautier, Victor Hugo, and Baudelaire all shine. But the English provide the greatest poetic music: along with Byron and Shelley, Christina Rossetti and Algernon Charles Swinburne are among the most technically finished artists in the book. Rossetti is represented by *Goblin Market* [complete] and "Repining"; Swinburne by "The Ballad of Dead Man's Bay" and "The Witch Mother."

Alert readers may note the absence certain well known verifiers—for example, William Blake (1757–1827), John Clare (1793–1864), George MacDonald (1824–1905), and Ambrose Bierce (1842–1914?). Some of these authors were deemed to be outside the scope of the book. It is a ticklish question as to what really "belongs" in the category supernatural poetry: the boundary with the poetry of mysticism (e.g., Blake) or of religious sentiment (e.g., MacDonald) is difficult to draw. Some will undoubtedly miss such material: by definition, "terror" is often characterized by "obscurity" or indeterminacy in its treatment of potentially horrible events.

There is, however, nothing like a "Western canon" of supernatural poetry; and Rutherford succeeds in both meeting his own goal and providing a satisfying frisson to the reader. Indeed, there are few more qualified to undertake such an effort as this: Rutherford is a distinguished neo-Romantic poet and scholar whose areas of specialty include Gothic, the supernatural, and classical mythology. One fine example of how story can act as a vehicle for weird atmosphere is Pushkin's poem, about a carriage ride into a blizzard that veers off into horror:

> The clouds whirl, the clouds scurry.
> The moon, unseen, lights up
> from above the flying snow.

> Gloom-ridden sky, gloom-ridden night:
> on my life, I can't find the way.
> We have no strength to go onward:
> there, look, our tracks again:
> we have gone in a full circle!
> The little bell is suddenly silent,
> in a fog so thick it cannot tremble.
> The horses stop. "What is that in the field?"

Similarly, the aforementioned William Bell Scott melds shudders with story in a powerful vignette of "Paracelsus":

> He was the aeronaut who flew
> Through skies becoming black like night,
> Above the rack and mountain range:
> Saw his own shadow on the white
> Cloud-world below that dazed his sight,
> And with his lapsing sense scarce knew
> That moving phantom, phantom strange,
> Was his own shadow. It was he
> Who lay in fever frenziedly,
> And chased the printed flowers that shed
> A mad confusion around his bed,
> Until at last they changed and past
> Into vermin around the dead.

The reader will find many more such pleasing terrors here. The book is well designed, and an excellent bibliography is provided. It is to be followed shortly by *Tales of Terror: The Supernatural Poem, Volume Two*, thus completing the venture begun by "Monk" Lewis in 1797. It will be a boon to both readers and critics to have a complete chronological record of supernatural poetry with uniform layout and editorial concept. There can be no real study of a genre such as supernatural fiction until accurate texts and representative works are easily accessible to scholars for detailed analysis and study; and this effort will undoubtedly supply the needed platform for such work, in addition to providing an entertaining and engrossing read for long after midnight.

Notes on Contributors

John Thomas Allen is a poet from New York. He has appeared frequently in poetry magazines. He has published a surrealist poetry collection, *Nouveau Midnight Sun* (Ravenna Press, 2014). Currently he is assembling another volume that harkens back to Aubrey Beardsley and the original "Yellow" decadent books.

David Barker has been a fan of weird literature all his life. Recently, his writings have appeared in *Fungi*, *Cyäegha*, and *Shoggoth.net*. In collaboration with W. H. Pugmire, David has had two books published by Dark Renaissance Books: *The Revenant of Rebecca Pascal* (2014) and *In the Gulfs of Dream and Other Lovecraftian Tales* (2015).

F. J. Bergmann writes poetry and speculative fiction, often simultaneously, appearing in *The 5-2 Crime Poetry*, *Black Treacle*, *Eschatology*, *Horror Garage*, and elsewhere, and functioning, so to speak, as editor of *Star*Line*, the journal of the Science Fiction Poetry Association, and poetry editor of *Mobius: The Journal of Social Change*.

Leigh Blackmore has written weird verse since age thirteen. He has lived in the Illawarra, New South Wales, Australia, for the last decade. He has edited *Terror Australis: Best Australian Horror* (1993) and *Midnight Echo 5* (2011) and written *Spores from Sharnoth & Other Madnesses* (2008). A nominee for SFPA's Rhysling Award (Best Long Poem), Leigh is also a four-time Ditmar Award nominee. He is currently compiling his second collection of fantastic verse and writing a thriller novel.

Adam Bolivar, a native of Boston, now residing in Portland, Oregon, has had his weird fiction and poetry appear in the pages of *Nameless*, the *Lovecraft eZine*, *Spectral Realms*, and Chaosium's *Steampunk Cthulhu* and *Atomic Age Cthulhu* anthologies. His first book, *The Fall of the House of Drake*, was published by Dunhams Manor Press in 2015.

Jason V Brock has been widely published in anthologies, online, comics, and magazines (*Weird Fiction Review*, S. T. Joshi's *Black Wings* series,

Fangoria, and many others). An award-winning filmmaker and publisher, he is also editor-in-chief of a website/print digest called [NameL3ss]. Along with his wife, Sunni, he is a herp, tech consultant, and health nut.

Pat Calhoun works from an old house in Santa Rosa, California, that he shares with his wife, three cats, and a large collection of fantasy books. He wrote a column, "Weird Words," about vintage fantasy comics, that ran for fifteen years in *Comic Book Marketplace* and currently writes for the *International Netsuke Society Journal.* He is also busy editing *Weird and Wondrous: An Anthology of Fantasy Poems,* and writing a few of them as well.

Frank Coffman is professor of English, journalism, and creative writing at Rock Valley College in Rockford, Illinois. His primary interests as a critic are in the rise and relevance of popular imaginative literature across the genres of adventures, detection and mystery, fantasy, horror and the supernatural, and science fiction. He has published several articles on these genres and is the editor of Robert E. Howard's *Selected Poems.*

Alicia Cole is a writer and editor in Atlanta. She is the co-founder of Priestess & Hierophant Perss, an active member of HWA, and the author of *Darkly Told: An Audio Chapbook.*

Margaret Curtis (MCA) is a witch, writer, artist, healer and activist, living in Wollongong, New South Wales, Australia. Published in magazines and anthologies, in print and online, she is the author of four collections of poetry. Her poem "A Deathless Love" appeared in *Midnight Echo* No 5 (AHWA, 2011).

Ashley Dioses is a writer of dark fiction and poetry from Southern California. She is currently working on her first book of weird poetry. Her poetry has appeared in *Weird Fiction Review, Spectral Realms, Xnoybis, Weirdbook, Gothic Blue Book,* Volume 5 (Burial Day Books, 2015), and elsewhere.

Poems by **Kendall Evans** have appeared in *Weird Tales, Analog, Asimov's*, and other magazines. His stories have appeared in *Amazing, Weirdbook, Fantastic*, and elsewhere. His novel *The Rings of Ganymede*, a ring cycle in the tradition of Wagner's operas and Tolkien's *Lord of the Rings*, is now available (Alban Lake Books, 2014).

Ian Futter began writing stories and poems in his childhood, but only lately has started to share them. One of his poems appears in Jason V Brock's anthology *The Darke Phantastique* (Cycatrix Press, 2014), and he continues to produce dark fiction for admirers of the surreal.

Liam Garriock is a writer, poet, and eternal disciple of Arthur Machen, Algernon Blackwood, William Hope Hodgson, Edgar Allan Poe, H. P. Lovecraft, and M. R. James, with an interest in the fantastic and esoteric side of life and anything that revolts against the prosaic. He lives in Edinburgh, Scotland.

Wade German's writings have appeared in journals such as *Fungi, Hypnos, Weirdbook, Weird Fiction Review*, and previous issues of *Spectral Realms*. His poetry has been nominated for the Pushcard, Rhysling, and Elgin awards and has received honorable mentions in Ellen Datlow's *Best Horror of the Year* anthologies. His collection *Dreams from a Black Nebula* was published by Hippocampus Press.

Alan Gullette is a poet and author whose work has appeared in three dozen amateur and small-press publications, including *Arkham Sampler, Crypt of Cthulhu, Cthulhu Codex, Etchings and Odysseys, Nyctalops*, and *Studies in Weird Fiction*. His omnibus *Intimations of Unreality* (Hippocampus Press, 2012) is in print.

Bram Stoker Award–nominated author **Chad Hensley** had his first book of poetry, *Embrace the Hideous Immaculate* (Raw Dog Screaming Press), published in May 2014. His recent poetry appearances include *Weirdbook, Cyäegha, Beyond the Cosmic Veil,* and *Spectral Realms*. His short story

"A Brush of Mammoth Wings" and poem "The Call" appear in *Nightgaunt* #3 in both French and English.

Charles Lovecraft has written verse since 1975, greatly inspired by H. P. Lovecraft. As publisher-editor he began P'rea Press in 2007 to publish weird and fantastic poetry, criticism and bibliography, and to keep traditional poetry forms alive (www.preapress.com). He has edited nineteen books. Charles has seen publication in *Nyctalops*, *Eldritch Tales*, *Pablo Lennis*, *Weird Fiction Review*, *Spectral Realms*, *Black Wings IV*, and *Beyond the Cosmic Threshold*.

Steven J. Mariconda is a leading authority on H. P. Lovecraft and has written critical essays on such writers as T. E. D. Klein and Ramsey Campbell. His essays on Lovecraft are gathered in *H. P. Lovecraft: Art, Artifact, and Reality* (Hippocampus Press, 2013). He is co-editor, with S. T. Joshi, of *Dreams of Fear: Poetry of Terror and the Supernatural* (Hippocampus Press, 2013).

Reiss McGuinness is a photographer and poet living in Bath. His poetry often deals with the politics and nature of the world, his haiku with hesitation, nostalgia, and mistakes. His haiku recently was featured in the Fringe Arts Bath festival. As Rabban, his photography practice involves dark and surreal images that portray estrangement and otherness.

John Mundy was born in a coal mining/railroading Pennsylvania town; discovered "The Raven" at five, Lovecraft and Beaumont at eight, and his fate was sealed. Three years ago, he was forced into physical inactivity from a leg injury that left him bored and depressed; and much to his surprise, he began to write poems and short stories. Thanks to his young and talented friend, Liam, he discovered *Spectral Realms* and decided to submit a few pieces. Everything after was a pleasant surprise!

D. L. Myers's poetry has appeared in previous issues of *Spectral Realms*. His influences include H. P. Lovecraft, Clark Ashton Smith, Robert E. Howard, George Sterling, Algernon Blackwood, and Arthur Machen. He dwells among the mist-shrouded hills and farms of the Skagit Valley in the Pacific Northwest with his partner and a pack of demon badger hounds.

William F. Nolan writes primarily in the science fiction, fantasy, and horror genres. Though best known as coauthor of the acclaimed dystopian science fiction novel *Logan's Run* (1967) with George Clayton Johnson, Nolan is the author of more than 2000 pieces (fiction, nonfiction, articles, and books), and has edited twenty-six anthologies in a career of more than fifty years. He received the Lifetime Achievement Award from the Horror Writers Association in 2010.

K. A. Opperman is a poet with a predilection for the strange, the Gothic, and the grotesque, continuing the macabre and fantastical tradition of such luminaries as Poe, Clark Ashton Smith, and H. P. Lovecraft. His first verse collection, *The Crimson Tome*, will was by Hippocampus Press in 2015.

Fred Phillips's first collection of poetry, *From the Cauldron*, was published by Hippocampus Press in 2010; a second collection, *Winds from Sheol*, is under way. He has been published in the *Cimmerian*, *Studies in the Fantastic*, *Weird Fiction Review*, and elsewhere.

Ann K. Schwader lives and writes in Colorado. Her most recent collectiona are *Twisted in Dream* (Hippocampus Press, 2011) and *Dark Energies* (P'rea Press, 2015). Her *Wild Hunt of the Stars* (Sam's Dot, 2010) was a Bram Stoker Award finalist. She is also a 2010 Rhysling Award winner and the Poet Laureate for NecronomiCon Providence 2015.

Darrell Schweitzer is a former editor of *Weird Tales*. His most recent book is a collection of Lovecraftian stories, *Awaiting Strange Gods*, from

Fedogan & Bremer. His two volumes of serious verse are *Groping toward the Light* and *Ghosts of Past and Future*. He is overdue for a third one.

John Shirley is the author of numerous novels and books of short stories. His latest novel is *Doyle After Death* (HarperCollins, 2013), a tale of Sir Arthur Conan Doyle in the afterlife. He won the Bram Stoker Award for his story collection *Black Butterflies*.

Donald Sidney-Fryer is the author of *Songs and Sonnets Atlantean* (Arkham House, 1971), *Emperor of Dreams: A Clark Ashton Smith Bibliography* (Donald M. Grant, 1978), *The Atlantis Fragments* (Hippocampus Press, 2009), and many other volumes. He has edited Smith's *Poems in Prose* (Arkham House, 1965) and written many books and articles on California poets. His autobiography *Hobgoblin Apollo* is forthcoming from Hippocampus Press in 2016.

Claire Smith holds an M.A. in English from the Open University. Her short stories have been published by Inkermen Press (2009). Her poetry has appeared in *Glevensis* (2013) and two previous issues of *Spectral Realms* (2014 and 2015). During 2015 her poems were also featured in the anthology *Fossil Lake II: The Refossiling* (2015) and the Alban Lake titles *Illumen* (2015) and *Trysts of Fate* (2015). She lives in Gloucestershire, UK.

Oliver Smith's writing has appeared in anthologies published by the Inkerman Press, Ex Occidente Press, and Dark Hall Press.

Christina Sng is a prolific writer of science fiction and horror poetry. She is a two-time Rhysling nominee and her work has received honorable mentions in *The Year's Best Fantasy and Horror*. Her latest book of poetry, *A Collection of Nightmares*, has been acquired by Raw Dog Screaming Press and is slated for late 2016.

Scott Thomas's poetry has appeared in numerous publications. He has also written ten books of fiction, including *The Sea of Ash, The Shadows of Flesh, The Garden of Ghosts,* and *Over the Darkening Fields*. His work appears with that of his brother Jeffrey Thomas in *Punktown: Shades of Grey*. Scott lives in New England.

Verse by Providence native **Jonathan Thomas** has consisted mostly of lyrics for country singer Angel Dean, Manhattan bands Escape by Ostrich and Fish & Roses, Swedish quartet scumCrown, and his own Septimania. His prose collections include *Midnight Call* (2008), *Tempting Providence* (2010), *Thirteen Conjurations* (2013), and *Dreams of Ys and Other Invisible Worlds* (2015), all from Hippocampus Press.

Kyla Lee Ward's latest release is *The Land of Bad Dreams* (P'rea Press, 2011), a collection of dark poetry. Her novel *Prismatic* (Lothian, 2006) won an Aurealis and her work on RPGs includes Demon the Fallen (White Wolf Games Studio, 2002). Short fiction, films, and plays—she's been there, as well as a whole lot of cemeteries.

M. F. Webb recently returned to writing from a two-decade long, journalism-induced hiatus. Her poetry has appeared in previous issues of *Spectral Realms,* and her fiction in *Latchkey Tales*. A Texas transplant, she has made her home in Seattle for the past seventeen years. Her great-great-great-grandmother was a Poe.

Mary Krawczak Wilson has written poetry, fiction, plays, articles, and essays. She was born in St. Paul, Minnesota, and moved to Seattle in 1991. Her most recent essay appeared in the *American Rationalist*.

Steven Withrow is a poet and storyteller from Cape Cod, Massachusetts. His poems have appeared in journals and anthologies for children, teens, and adults. He has taught at Rhode Island School of Design, on the hill in Providence near where Lovecraft lived, and at Suffolk University in Boston.

www.ingramcontent.com/pod-product-compliance
Lightning Source LLC
Chambersburg PA
CBHW060802050426
42449CB00008B/1502